THE McGRAW-HILL HANDBOOK OF DISTANCE LEARNING

THE McGRAW-HILL HANDBOOK OF DISTANCE LEARNING

Alan G. Chute

Director
Lucent Technologies
Center for Excellence in Distance Learning

Melody M. Thompson

Assistant Director, World Campus
The Pennsylvania State University

Burton W. Hancock

Director
Nationwide Insurance
Performance Improvement Organization

McGraw-Hill
New York   San Francisco   Washington, D.C.   Auckland   Bogotá
Caracas   Lisbon   London   Madrid   Mexico City   Milan   Montreal
New Delhi   San Juan   Singapore
Sydney   Tokyo   Toronto

Library of Congress Cataloging-in-Publication Data

Chute, Alan G.
        The McGraw-Hill handbook of distance learning / Alan G. Chute,
    Melody M. Thompson, Burton W. Hancock.
            p.   cm.
        Includes bibliographical references and index.
        ISBN 0-07-012028-5
        I. Distance education—United States.   2. Information technology-
    United States   3. Computer assisted instruction—United States.
    I. Thompson, Melody M.   II. Hancock, Burton W.   III. Title.
    IV. Title: Handbook of distance learning.
    LC5805.C58   1998
    371.3'5'0973—dc21   98-45143
                                                                        CIP

McGraw-Hill

A Division of The McGraw·Hill Companies

    2 3 4 5 6 7 8 9 0   AGM/AGM   9 0 3 2 1 0 9

ISBN 0-07-012028-5

*The sponsoring editor for this book was Richard Narramore, the
editing supervisor was Caroline R. Levine, and the production
supervisor was Clare Stanley. It was set in Fairfield by Ron Painter of
McGraw-Hill's Professional Book Group composition unit.*

Printed and bound by Quebecor/Martinsburg.

McGraw-Hill books are available at special quantity discounts to
use as premiums and sales promotions, or for use in corporate
training programs. For more information, please write to the
Director of Special Sales, McGraw-Hill, 11 West 19th Street, New
York, NY 10011. Or contact your local bookstore.

This book is printed on recycled, acid-free paper containing
a minimum of 50% recycled, de-inked fiber.

CONTENTS

CHAPTER 7. PROGRAM DESIGN, DELIVERY, AND EVALUATION   125

ACKNOWLEDGMENTS

We owe an enormous debt to the hundreds of people who have helped us learn the art, science, and practice of distance learning. There are too many people to list them individually. Instead, we choose to collectively acknowledge those colleagues who have shaped our understanding and appreciation of distance learning. Thus, we acknowledge the many professionals we have worked with at AT&T, Ernst & Young, Indiana University, Lucent Technologies, Nationwide Insurance, Penn State University, the United States Army, the University of South Dakota, and the University of Wisconsin. And, finally, we want to acknowledge our parents—the source of our initial learning—and our families, who support us and contribute to our learning every day.

Alan G. Chute
Melody M. Thompson
Burton W. Hancock

THE McGRAW-HILL
HANDBOOK OF
DISTANCE LEARNING

THE TIME IS RIGHT FOR DISTANCE LEARNING

At a time when learning is coming to be recognized as a critical component in an organization's success, new organizational structures are challenging the way organizations support learning. Traditional centralized classroom learning is losing value in organizations that are becoming more decentralized and more global. Simultaneously, educators and trainers are reexamining the entire learning process—when, how, and where learning occurs.

The advent of alternative approaches to work, such as telecommuting, has increased the complexity of the relationship between work and learning. In the past learning was an event to be experienced in a classroom, completed, and certified, but today learning is considered a continuous process. The challenge for an organization is to make learning available to its members when and where the need arises. The essence of this challenge is reflected in the words of Arie DeGeus of Royal Dutch/Shell Oil as cited in Peter Senge's *The Fifth Discipline:*

> The ability to learn faster than your competitors may be the only sustainable competitive advantage.[1]

Increasingly, the challenge of learning faster than one's competitors is being met through distance learning applications. Corporations are using video, audio, computer, and Internet distance learning technologies to train and retrain their globally deployed work-forces. Some common training and retraining needs that are being addressed by distance learning applications include

- New product and policy information
- Job skills training and retraining
- Advanced professional education
- Management development courses
- Customer education

This book is written for people who by choice or necessity want to help their organizations implement distance learning programs. You may work in business, in higher education, or for the government. You may be a trainer, a human resources professional, or a teacher. You may be an information technology manager responsible for setting up the infrastructure that makes distance learning possible for your organization, an instructional designer charged with the development of a course to prepare a geographically dispersed sales force to implement new company directives, or an educational officer directed by your organization's leadership to implement an employee education and enrichment program on a limited budget.

If one of these descriptions fits you, this book will be a valuable resource. *The McGraw-Hill Handbook of Distance Learning* will introduce you to the ways in which distance learning solutions can be applied to save an organization money and dramatically increase the number of learners it serves. The *Handbook* offers practical advice to help get an organization started in distance learning or improve an existing distance learning program in the following specific areas:

- Getting buy-in and support from all stakeholders, including management, instructors, and learners
- Creating a cross-functional team responsible for recommending the best approach to distance learning for your organization
- Assessing the costs involved and getting financial backing from management and other sources
- Choosing the most appropriate technologies for your training and educational delivery needs
- Retraining your instructors to comfortably and effectively design and deliver distance learning activities in this new environment
- Providing needed support for distance learners
- Increasing student satisfaction and improving learning outcomes through program evaluation and improvement

- Determining when your distance learning system should be expanded
- Keeping up with technological advances for your distance learning system

WHY BUSINESS AND INDUSTRY NEED DISTANCE LEARNING

The only constant in today's business environment is change. Nearly every American business is facing shrinking budgets and scarce resources, yet the competition is fiercer than ever before, forcing businesses to find ways to get higher-quality products to the marketplace faster and with fewer resources. And with the ease of worldwide travel and communication, more and more companies are "going global."

The number of skilled employees needed cannot come from a pool of new people; skilled employees have to be current workers who develop their skills through training and retraining. Not only do the skills of low-skill level employees need to be strengthened, employees in jobs requiring high skill levels need continuous retraining. Knowing how to do today's jobs is no longer good enough. As technology explodes and reshapes the workplace, today's job skills will become obsolete as tomorrow's jobs require a whole new set of worker skills. All these changes require changes in the way workers are trained and retrained.

EDUCATION NEEDS DISTANCE LEARNING TOO

The business sector is not the only area of society that is experiencing changes. America's universities, colleges, community colleges, and public schools also are facing many challenges.

HIGHER EDUCATION

With the baby boom generation no longer providing a seemingly endless supply of students, universities and colleges must find new, nontraditional markets for their services. Increasingly, postsecondary learners will speak multiple languages, live all over the world, and be reached on remote campuses, in government and business work-places, and directly in their homes. Not only must institutions devel-op ways to distribute their basic product—education—to both tradi-tional and new learner populations, they must do so with shrinking budgets. Distance learning is a way to meet the changing higher edu-cation needs of a dynamic and complex society flexibly.

Like business, education is being influenced by the transforma-tion into an information society. Ideas about what is "educationally appropriate" are changing as educators work to develop procedures and strategies that will help students deal effectively with the new learning environment. Modern information and communications technologies can help educators meet the dual challenge of (1) giv-ing students the tools needed to access a virtually unlimited array of information and (2) developing and teaching the processes and pro-cedures that allow learners to go beyond information access to transform these raw materials into personally and socially useful knowledge.

Some of the programs that are being delivered by higher educa-tion institutions through distance learning include

- Undergraduate and graduate courses
- Certificate and degree programs
- Continuing education
- Staff development and in-service training

ELEMENTARY AND SECONDARY EDUCATION

Distance learning applications are being implemented in elementary and secondary education to improve access to instruction and edu-cational resources. The raw material of learning—information and experts—is distributed around the globe. Distance learning tech-nologies serve as the critical connectors between a school and the outside world by linking teachers and learners at multiple sites and making human and informational resources widely available.

Educational technologies offer teachers tools to structure learn-ing environments that encourage both individual and collaborative educational activities. The power and flexibility of distance learning technologies offer new and enhanced ways to incorporate active and interactive learning experiences into curricula at all educational lev-els to most appropriately meet the needs of an increasingly diverse population of learners.

Some of the distance learning applications that are being implemented in the kindergarten-through-twelfth-grade environment include

- Advanced placement high school courses
- Curriculum enrichment programs
- Virtual field trips
- Networking with students in other cultures
- Staff development

Later in this book we will provide examples of innovative and successful distance learning applications in a variety of educational contexts.

TEN WAYS ORGANIZATIONS CAN BENEFIT FROM DISTANCE LEARNING

In 1997–1998 corporations will spend over $60 billion for all aspects of corporate education and training. We believe that a sizable chunk of this money will be wasted on travel costs and inefficient or outmoded approaches to delivering workforce education.

Distance learning can help. In 1997 a wide variety of user groups spent over $1 billion on distance learning systems. Using distance learning systems, trainers and educators are delivering more training to more people on more subjects with greater effectiveness, and in a much more cost-effective way, than ever before. The decision to implement distance learning can be a powerful step toward achieving cost benefits and productivity improvements in an organization.

Here are 10 benefits reported by organizations that have successfully implemented distance learning programs:

1. Distance learning increases the impact and productivity of dollars invested in training and education programs.
2. Distance learning reduces travel costs and makes time formerly spent traveling available for more productive purposes.
3. Distance learning allows the training of more people, more often, in short learning sessions that are easier to schedule and coordinate.

4. Distance learning is scaleable; it offers the ability to add students and instructors as needed without incurring significant additional expenses.

5. Distance learning programs deliver a consistent message that can quickly be disseminated companywide to ensure the consistency and quality of the work performed by employees or students.

6. Distance learning provides for real-time updates and just-in-time information access.

7. Distance learning programs can be delivered to work or home sites that are convenient for students.

8. Distance learning offers live interactive programs that can be delivered to multiple networked sites for group learning and collaborative problem solving.

9. Distance learning programs are learner-centered, affording students more control of the pacing, sequencing, and style of interaction of the learning experience.

10. Distance learning offers easy access to learning resources and remote experts internal and external to the organization.

TECHNOLOGIES AND APPLICATIONS

To effectively plan and implement distance learning solutions, you first need to understand the technologies involved. Generally speaking, systems are based on telephone, computer, video, or Internet technologies or on some combination of those technologies. These categories and the distance learning systems they support are discussed in detail in Chaps. 2 and 3.

BASIC TERMINOLOGY: FROM ANALOG TO WORLD WIDE WEB

Distance learning is a new approach to traditional and familiar activities: education and training. However, some of the terminology of distance learning may not seem familiar. To provide a frame of reference for the discussions of technologies and activities that make up this book, we have provided a glossary of terms used in planning and implementing distance learning programs. If you become somewhat familiar with these terms, you will have an easier time understanding discussions about distance learning and choosing appropriate education and training solutions. You can find this material in the Glossary.

IT'S EVERYWHERE! EXAMPLES OF SUCCESSFUL APPLICATIONS IN BUSINESS, EDUCATION, GOVERNMENT, AND THE MILITARY

The power and flexibility of distance learning technologies make them suitable for meeting a wide range of education and training needs. Below we offer a few examples of ways in which educational institutions and other organizations have successfully applied distance learning solutions.

CORPORATE TRAINING VIA SATELLITE BROADCAST

Ford Motor Company needed to quickly quadruple its dealer training output. They already had 162 instructors, but demand for training among the United States and international dealer trainee population was growing too rapidly to be met in traditional ways—building additional training centers and hiring more instructors for face-to-face training. Ford instead decided to expand dramatically its broadcast satellite network FORDSTAR to 5200 locations in the United States, 650 in Canada, 135 in Mexico, and another 300 in Australia. In 1997 FORDSTAR provided 14,000 hours of programming in the United States alone, reaching 400,000 students with 5000 classes. The advantages of the FORDSTAR distance learning solution include

1. Learners can *interact* with a live instructor and guest subject matter experts without having to travel.
2. *Speed* of training delivery is several times that of traditional classroom-based training.
3. *Reach* of training to even the most remote associates is possible at much lower cost.
4. *Dealer savings* is achieved through partial replacement of expensive, time-consuming travel to central training sites.

PENN STATE'S WORLD CAMPUS: MEETING THE NEEDS OF WORKING PROFESSIONALS

Penn State's World Campus (http://www.worldcampus.psu.edu/) extends programs of the university to working professionals in a number of fields, including turfgrass management, noise control engineering, and chemical dependency counseling. Using a variety of interactive technologies, Penn State offers flexible, worldwide educational access to those who, because of geographic isolation or the pressures and constraints of their work and life circumstances, are unable or choose not to attend classes as resident students. Instructors use a robust mixture of presentational and interactive teaching methods and distance learning technologies—computer conferencing, videoconferencing, CD-ROM, the World Wide Web, and print—to offer students educational experiences that do not try to duplicate traditional classroom instruction but instead create a new kind of learning environment that meets the lifelong learning needs of today's adult students.

ELEMENTARY AND SECONDARY DISTANCE LEARNING NETWORKS

Elementary and secondary schools are using a variety of delivery strategies to increase access to and expand the range of the courses they offer. For example, satellite video technologies are used to deliver Japanese-language instruction from Nebraska to thousands of students nationwide. Computer conferencing links elementary students in Minnesota to their international counterparts for role-playing activities that focus on issues of international importance. The Indiana Higher Education Telecommunications System delivers higher-level courses such as advanced mathematics and foreign languages to about 70 schools within that state through a fiber-optic network, while in Texas migrant students receive instruction in algebra through a low-cost audioconferencing system. In Canada a combination of technologies that includes print, radio, fax, computers, and television is used to deliver high school instruction to students living on reserves.

SATELLITE BROADCASTING FOR SCHOOLS AND TRAINING CENTERS

The launching of AT&T's Telstar 4 family of satellites marked the beginning of the educational neighborhood in the sky. Today Telstar 401 delivers information and lifelong learning opportunities to schools, universities, businesses, and other learning centers across the nation.

The Public Broadcasting Service (PBS) provides nationwide educational programs such as PBS MATHLINE and the Adult Learning Satellite Service (ALSS), which offers undergraduate-level courses and resources programming to over 2000 colleges, universities, hospitals, and other organizations equipped with satellite-receive capabilities throughout the country. The Business Channel, a service of PBS's ALSS, offers specialized training and resource programming to this nation's small and midsize businesses, large corporations, and continuing education and business institutes in colleges and universities.

GOVERNMENT DISTANCE LEARNING PROGRAMS

Faced with reductions in personnel and funding brought about by downsizing, the federal government and the U.S. Department of Defense (DOD) have embraced distance learning as an important strategy to satisfy their training and retraining requirements. Within the federal government, the Army, Navy, and Air Force; the Federal Aviation Administration (FAA); the U.S. Department of Energy (DOE); and the U.S. Environmental Protection Agency (EPA), among others, have initiated aggressive distance learning programs by constructing satellite network systems under the Federal Telecommunications System 2000 (FTS 2000) contract.

An interservice network called the Defense Commercial Telecommunications Network (DCTN) provides satellite-delivered courses from broadcast studios to hundreds of downlink sites across the country. By delivering education and training courses at a distance, the DCTN is offering the military services a cost-effective way to distribute training to personnel in all 50 states. DOD has increased productivity through reduced travel time, the distribution of time-sensitive information, and simultaneous communication with immediate feedback.

These are just a few examples of institutions and organizations that are successfully meeting their educational and training needs through distance learning. As we discuss the various aspects of distance learning, we will share other examples of innovative distance learning applications in a wide variety of contexts.

As these examples show, distance learning applications are appropriate in almost any learning environment. When properly planned and implemented, they can be a powerful force in realizing the goal of high-quality lifelong learning.

KEYS TO SUCCESS

Successful distance learning programs do not just happen; they result from thoughtful and informed planning and implementation. Attention to the following issues is necessary to ensure the success of a distance learning initiative. Each of these points is discussed in detail later in the book, but it is important to keep them in mind as you begin to explore various distance learning solutions.

1. *Determine your needs up front.* Before implementation begins, set up a cross-functional team made up of trainers, instructional designers, telecommunications staff, and end users. Identify in advance any concerns or needs related to the training process or technology and address them before delivering the first distance learning program.

2. *Look to distance learning as a way to revitalize and innovate the existing training program.* For example, multimedia and the World Wide Web can be incorporated easily to stimulate and reinforce your learning goals.

3. *Start using a multilevel evaluations approach* (e.g., student satisfaction, learning transfer, improved job performance, financial impact). Multilevel evaluation is a fundamental part of the cost justification for distance learning. In addition to examining how employees react to the program, evaluate how the program is influencing actual job performance through follow-up surveys, interviews, and the like.

4. *Keep the focus on what you are learning, not on the technology that is helping you learn.* Discussions at the end of a distance learning program should center on the course content rather than the technology used for delivery. Make sure the participants are comfortable with the technology early in the program so that they can concentrate on the learning process.

5. *Market your distance learning program internally and externally.* Tell people within your business unit about your achievements with distance learning and then spread the news to other business units through internal newsletters, word of mouth, and other communication vehicles.

6. *Use on-site coordination.* Provide an on-site coordinator at each remote location. The remote coordinator should be skilled in using the technology and setting up advance testing of all the

equipment. The coordinator's other responsibilities can include distributing course materials, greeting participants as they arrive, and providing a contact number in case problems occur.

7. *Obtain local field manager commitment.*   Before delivering distance learning programs to remote sites, get a commitment from the local field manager and the on-site coordinator that the room will be reserved for the length of the session. Also, make sure the participants will not be interrupted by their regular job responsibilities during the training program.

8. *Make sure the instructors are well trained.*   Provide thorough training for instructors in distance learning presentation skills. Take advantage of training workshops. As instructors become experienced, they will be able to mentor new trainers in regard to their distance delivery.

9. *Design programs specifically for distance learning.*   Careful planning is essential in designing a distance learning program. A good balance between human interaction and the use of technical "props" will enhance the learning experience. Charts, graphics, role-playing, case studies, brainstorming, and question-and-answer sessions stimulate the learning process and encourage better participation and learning recall.

10. *Use reliable equipment.*   Dependable equipment ensures the most successful distance learning experience. Be sure to purchase your technology from an established vendor.

If we have convinced you that the time is right for distance learning in *your* organization, we invite you to join us as we move into Chap. 1 for an in-depth discussion of helping others in your organization see the value of distance learning solutions.

NOTES

1. Senge, P. 1990. *The fifth discipline: The art and practice of the learning organization.* New York: Doubleday Currency.

CONVINCING YOUR ORGANIZATION OF THE NEED FOR DISTANCE LEARNING

Employee development is critical to the strategic value of all businesses that compete in the global business environment. In other words, learning in the workplace is central to organizational transformation and to sustaining an organization's competitive advantage.

Although traditional training department structures and classroom delivery of learning worked well in the past, they are neither flexible enough nor powerful enough to support all of today's educational and training needs. Rapid change is sweeping over global business: Intense global competition, imbalances in wage and production policies between nations, the infusion of new technologies, and increasing customer demands for quality are occurring at the same time that labor and financial resources are shrinking. This combination of circumstances puts unprecedented pressure on organizations to be more efficient and effective. The bottom line is that *no organization can remain the same and expect to survive.* Traditional organizations resist change; it is up to you to persuade management and users to adopt a distance learning solution.

THE ONLY CONSTANT IS CHANGE: KNOWLEDGE NEEDS IN RAPIDLY CHANGING ORGANIZATIONAL ENVIRONMENTS

In the 1980s organizations focused on reducing costs, automating production, and reengineering their business processes. These actions were taken to satisfy customer needs and improve an organization's competitive position. The results of these initiatives were lower operating costs and improved productivity for the organization. Organizations did not, however, experience significant improvements in their competitive position in the marketplace. Essentially, each of these strategies is easily replicable by *any* organization, thus eroding the competitive advantage. However, organizations that took these actions to improve their operations *and focused on the development of the workforce* did see a significant improvement in their competitive standing.

From the experiences of the 1980s there evolved an understanding of the importance of organizational learning. Robert Kaplan and David Norton[1] have proposed that in addition to traditional financial, customer satisfaction, and business process measures, organizations need to consider measuring organizational learning. The Balanced Scorecard approach proposed by Kaplan and Norton directs attention to learning and growth as the basis for the future success of an organization. Adequate investment in an organization's people, processes, and infrastructure is critical to long-term success.

The new organization must be highly flexible and able to deploy new teams of employees in continuously changing configurations as market conditions dictate. This goal cannot be reached without the support of an efficient and effective—and therefore continually evolving—workplace training structure. In many cases that entails training programs that incorporate distance learning.

THE ADVANTAGES OF DISTANCE LEARNING IN THE WORK ENVIRONMENT

All the trends we have discussed so far point to the conclusion that organizations that want to stay competitive need to find more effective and efficient ways to train and educate their workforces in a rapidly changing range of skills. However, it is well known that organizations and institutions are reluctant to adopt a new approach to anything, including teaching and training, without some compelling arguments for doing so. For this reason, the first step in getting started with a distance learning program is usually to understand and convince others of the advantages of this form of delivery. Luckily, there is plenty of evidence to support claims of distance learning effectiveness for many educational and training needs. Both scholarly research and practical experience have shown that distance learning is educationally effective, offers business value, and is in many cases more cost-effective than are other approaches.

IT'S EDUCATIONALLY EFFECTIVE

A question that often arises in relation to distance learning is, How effective is it? Because distance education and training does not *look* like traditional instruction—and because its supporters often stress benefits such as cost-effectiveness and increased access—people often wonder whether they may have to compromise on educational effectiveness to get these benefits.

For almost 70 years educators, psychologists, and other experts have studied various forms of distance teaching and learning in order to answer this question. After looking first at correspondence instruction and then at instruction using technologies such as radio, television, and interactive audioconferencing, videoconferencing, and computer conferencing, these researchers have overwhelmingly reported that *there is no significant difference in the achievement of students in well-designed distance learning programs and the achievement of those in traditional face-to-face programs, based on standard performance measures.* This result has been reported for learners at different educational levels, for many subject areas, and in a variety of contexts. Examples of the groups studied include elementary, secondary, undergraduate, and graduate students; working professionals; and military personnel. The subject areas represented in effectiveness research have included foreign languages, mathematics, teacher education, laboratory science, business, computer science, military skills, and nursing. Two publications that are useful in documenting the effectiveness of distance learning are *The Effects of Distance Learning*,[2] a review of selected literature on the effectiveness of distance learning over a period of more than 30 years, and "The no-significant difference phenonmenon,"[3] a report on the results from over 250 research studies on distance learning.

The weight of practical and research evidence has largely dispelled concerns about the potential educational effectiveness of distance learning methods. Distance education is recognized as a viable means of teaching and learning that offers a variety of benefits to both learners and organizations.

IT OFFERS BUSINESS VALUE

A question many companies face is related to the value of the knowledge held by their employees. Today's source of wealth is not material; instead, it is information and knowledge applied to work to create value. Estimates of the value of the intellectual assets of a company typically range from three to nine times a company's book value.

How can you know the value of information and knowledge in your organization? One way to approach this question is to modify a traditional accounting measure of the time value of money. The first premise is that the value of current knowledge depreciates over time because of changing conditions and the rapid increase of new knowledge. The second assumption is that the value of knowledge today will be higher in the future if it is applied to the acquisition of additional knowledge, that is, if it is applied to learning.

Continuing with this accounting metaphor, two conditions of the information age relate to human intellectual capital. First, *unless current knowledge is refreshed, it loses value,* like money hidden in a mattress. Second, *the faster information and knowledge are distributed to people in an organization the greater is the opportunity for that information and knowledge to create additional learning.*

Because information and knowledge are increasing so rapidly, organizations find themselves challenged to distribute this "wealth" to their people quickly to protect current knowledge assets or increase their value through organizational learning. Distance learning can facilitate the distribution of information and knowledge to develop a "learning organization."

The various capabilities of distance learning add to an organization's capacity to distribute knowledge and enhance its competitive position in the marketplace. Whether delivered by videoconferencing, computer-based training, Web-based instruction, or other technologies or combinations of technologies, distance learning can get information and knowledge to people anywhere and at any time.

IT'S COST-EFFECTIVE

The cost-effectiveness of a distance learning system depends on several factors, including the comparative costs of traditional and distance learning systems, savings from reduced travel for instructors and students, and the potential for increased enrollments over a larger geographic area. However, numbers (of either dollars or learners) are not the only consideration. Any determination of the cost-effectiveness of distance learning (or any other systems, for that matter) must be based on a comparison of cost and educational value. To paraphrase Richard Hezel, the basic question is not, Does distance learning cost more or less than traditional education or training? but rather, Is the educational outcome worth the cost?[4] Many businesses are answering a resounding yes to this question as a result of the significant cost savings, increased productivity, and opportunities for continuing and collaborative professional development realized through distance learning approaches.

Significant Cost Savings.   The potential financial impact of distance learning can be significant. Distance learning can provide a cost-effective solution to the most demanding training and educational needs. With distance learning, companies can deliver training in traditional group learning environments using a range of audio, audiographic, or group video solutions; alternatively, programs can be delivered right to the desktop via Internet technologies. Students at multiple sites can be easily connected using audio bridges, video multipoint conferencing units (MCUs), or network-based multipoint call-bridging capability. Consider the following cost-saving examples for representative training programs. (The technologies mentioned in these examples are discussed in detail in Chaps. 2 and 3.)

This first example compares the costs of different delivery methods for a half-day program to introduce new product and service knowledge. A program delivered by distance learning video technology to four sites with 10 salespeople per site results in considerable cost savings compared with "suitcase" delivery, where the instructor travels to the student sites, or centralized delivery, where the students travel to a central site. Assume conservatively that average airfare is $400 per trip with $100 per diem for expenses. It costs $2000 if the instructor travels to remote sites and $20,000 if the 40 students travel to a central site.

By comparison, a typical Integrated Services Digital Network (ISDN) video distance learning session costs $1500 in network charges and video bridging services per program. There is a one-time equipment cost of less than $3000 for desktop video units, and group video systems can cost less than $10,000 per site. The desktop video units pay for themselves in the first offering of the program; the group video systems can pay for themselves in two offerings or less.

A second example compares the typical costs of delivering a professional skills development training program. A three-day program delivered to three sites with eight employees per site realizes significant savings over the centralized delivery of instruction. A typical video distance learning three-day session would cost $7000 in network charges and video MCU services compared with $16,000 if the 24 students traveled to a central site. These are travel costs projections that do not take into consideration the lost time and productivity expenses associated with students or instructors traveling to training sites.

A third and a fourth example of the cost effectiveness of distance training are cited in a report published in the *Educational and Training Technology International Journal.*[5] That report summarizes a year of cost-saving data for courses and update programs delivered by distance learning at the AT&T University of Sales Excellence.

In 1989 AT&T reported cost avoidance figures for courses delivered via audiographic technologies. The assumption was made that students would have had to travel to a centralized training center in Cincinnati to receive this training if there had not been a distance learning alternative.

During that year 3650 students attended distance-delivered sessions (with an average course length of seven hours) of courses in the training curricula. An average round-trip airfare of $400 and a per diem cost of $100 for lodging and daily expenses resulted in a total travel cost avoidance per student of $500 per course. The total cost avoidance for the 3650 students was $1,825,000.

The cost avoidance for travel is offset somewhat by the telephone and bridging expenses associated with distance learning. A typical distance learning course at the AT&T University of Sales Excellence had one host instructor site and four remote student sites. This network configuration resulted in expenses for five lines and five ports on the bridge. Bridging expenses were based on AT&T Alliance Teleconferencing Services. Additional capital investments in equipment were not considered in these calculations, since the company's existing personal computers (PCs) were used; only operating expenses were included. Using these figures, the total network expenses for the 170 distance learning sessions were $217,600. Subtracting the network expenses from the cost avoidance figure produced a travel cost avoidance of $1,607,400, or $440 per student.

Travel cost avoidance was only part of the actual savings realized from distance learning. Substantial employee productivity savings also occurred through the reemployment of nonproductive time spent traveling, waiting in airports, and catching up on work back at the home location. The assumption that the average nonproductive time was six hours per student produced a total productivity gain of

$525,600, or $144 per student. Adding these productivity savings to the earlier savings in travel costs produced a total cost avoidance of $2,133,000, or $584 per student.

Another example addresses cost avoidance for the one-hour audio update programs offered on AT&T's National Teletraining Network. In 1989 over 69,000 students attended audio update programs. Two assumptions were made in doing these calculations. First, it would not be practical to have students from the 350 field locations travel to Cincinnati to participate in a 60-minute training session. Therefore, each presenter would have had to travel to a minimum of 70 major sites to reach 90 percent of the students. Second, the students would utilize ground transportation, not air transportation, at the remote locations to attend a training session in one of the 70 major sites. This eliminated the need to compute additional student travel expenses. If each presenter had traveled to 70 sites, the costs incurred would have been $400 for airfare and $100 for local expenses at each site; the travel cost for each presenter would have been $35,000 per program. For the 254 update programs presented in 1989, the travel cost avoided amounted to $8,890,000.

The cost analysis for the update programs also accounts for the expenses associated with the operation of the network. The cost of all the long-distance calls made to Cincinnati from the remote locations was $278,000. A dedicated bridge located in Cincinnati was used to connect all the sites for the programs. The expense incurred in 1989 for the leasing and operation of the dedicated bridge was $311,000. The expenses incurred for faxing, mailing, and photocopying the handout materials used for the programs in 1989 was $61,000. The net cost avoidance for the 1989 audio update programs was $8,250,000, or $32,480 per program.

Distance learning solutions have produced significant travel cost avoidance for AT&T. Major savings were realized for both full courses and update programs delivered at a distance.

The information presented here substantiates the fact that distance learning is a cost-efficient alternative to the face-to-face delivery of training. With the advent of Internet-based distance learning technologies, the costs of delivery are becoming even lower, making distance learning an increasingly attractive alternative to the face-to-face delivery of instruction.

Increased Productivity. There are different models for determining the cost-effectiveness of distance learning. The most frequently used model is travel cost avoidance, which was detailed above. The difference between travel costs and distance learning costs—such as capital investment in facilities, equipment, and telecommunications—yields one measure of how cost-effective distance learning can be.

Another way to calculate cost-effectiveness is associated with productivity gains. This measure assigns a value to the effort made by an individual and assumes that because that individual was able to remain on the job, there have been gains in productivity.

Another, more difficult measure is the value employees receive from distance learning that they could not receive otherwise. This assumes that the learning has an impact on the bottom line of an organization. Measures of bottom line impact include increased revenues, reduced operating expenses, and increased customer satisfaction that results in increased sales.

LOW-COST ONGOING NETWORKING WITH COLLEAGUES

One characteristic of today's powerful and flexible communications technologies is their ability to link learners to widely distributed information resources, including the just-in-time technical resources needed to solve immediate problems in the workplace. However, knowledge resides not only in various information resources or databases but also within the minds of other professionals working in a given field. One of the most valuable attributes of distance learning technologies is their ability to link people *to each other* for purposes of professional growth and development.

The professionals working in your business or organization represent a gold mine of knowledge and expertise developed through "situated practice." Through collaborative interaction, this expertise can be shared, critiqued, and refined to improve an organization's work practices. Distance learning technologies allow the formation of "communities of practice" that are not limited by the need to meet at the same time or in the same location.

Technology-based communities of practice have been reported in both education and business. For example, educators have used this mechanism to "meet" and discuss issues before, during, and after professional conferences. Other practicing professionals in widely diverse fields such as prison education, technology-based human resources development, and media design and development have joined together across distances for collaborative professional networking and problem solving through distance learning technologies.[6]

CASE STUDY: JUST-IN-TIME LEARNING AND NETWORKING

The JITOL (Just-in-Time Open Learning)[7] program is a good example of a professional development approach that integrates timely access to information with collaborative networking between colleagues in the advanced learning technology field. Careful planning and implementation of this project, which was funded by the European Community's DELTA program, has produced a structure of communication and learning that continuously enhances the growth and development of an entire professional work community.

The JITOL program goes well beyond typical just-in-time solutions, which often focus narrowly on access to information. Although an important aspect of the program is teaching the participants to find and retrieve information to apply to specific problems of practice, another component emphasizes the value of discussion and collaboration among colleagues through computer conferencing.

The underlying goal of the JITOL project is the linking of just-in-time, research-based, professionally relevant knowledge to the everyday knowledge of working professionals. In this way, current practice improves and new working practices evolve through collaboration. The project uses computer-mediated communication (CMC) to develop and maintain a community of practice within which colleagues share and refine their practices and knowledge. JITOL is a project that goes beyond teaching the participants to solve immediate, and often limited, problems to stimulate learning and the construction of a community of learning and practice. As such, this project is an excellent example of the powerful and innovative solutions distance learning can offer for workplace education and training needs.

NOTES

1. Kaplan, R. S., and D. P. Norton, 1996. *The balanced scorecard: Translating strategy into action.* New York: Doubleday Currency.

2. Moore, M., and M. Thompson. 1997. *The effects of distance learning,* rev. ed. ACSDE Research Monograph 15. University Park, PA: American Center for the Study of Distance Education, The Pennsylvania State University.

3. Russell, T. (compiler). 1997. The no significant difference phenomenon. NB TeleEducation (on-line) (http://tenb.mta.ca/phenom/).

4. Hezel, R. T. Cost effectiveness for interactive distance education and telecommunicated training. In *Proceedings of the Eighth Annual Conference on Distance Teaching and Learning,* Madison: University of Wisconsin–Madison, 75–78.

5. *Educational and Training Technology International Journal,* 1990, vol. 27, no. 3.

6. Thompson, M. 1996. Distance delivery of graduate-level teacher education: Beyond parity claims. *Journal of Continuing Higher Education* 44(3):29–34.

7. Goodyear, P. 1995. Situated action and distributed knowledge: A JITOL perspective on EPSS. *Innovations in Education and Training International* 32(1):45–55.

AN OVERVIEW OF AUDIO, VIDEO, AND COMPUTER-BASED DISTANCE LEARNING TECHNOLOGIES

The technologies that support distance learning continually increase in number, complexity, and power. As the options increase, so does the difficulty in choosing appropriate distance learning solutions for particular educational and training needs. This section provides an overview of some of the more traditional or familiar options for distance learning delivery, including those based on audio, video, and data (computer) technologies. Chapter 3 discusses additional distance learning options, particularly those based on the Internet and the World Wide Web.

Figure 2-1 provides a summary of all the technologies and technology combinations discussed in Chaps. 3 and 4. These distance learning solutions span a wide range, from one-way audio broadcasts where students can only listen to the instructor to two-way interactive multimedia telecollaboration in which all the sites can see and hear each other and simultaneously collaborate in a shared data communications medium.

We do not believe that there is a single "silver bullet" distance technology that is ideal for all educational and training needs and learner requirements. One size does not fit all! Instead, a multiple media approach is what we have implemented in our own organiza-

TECHNOLOGIES

Type of Interaction	Audio	Data	Video	Audio/Data Examples	Video/Data Examples	Audio/Video Examples	Audio/Video/Data
One-way	Audiotape, radio broadcast, dial access audio resources	Computer-based training (CBT), videotext, bulletin boards, Internet	Videotape, video-broadcast. One-way video, Video on Demand (VOD)	Audio programs supplemented by on-line access to World Wide Web (WWW) resources	Video programs supplemented by CBT, video-text, WWW resources	Audio or video programs supplemented by audiotapes or videotapes, dial access, audio, VOD	Multimedia programming
Two-way asynchronous ("time-delayed")	Voice mail	E-mail, Internet	Video messaging	Audio programs supplemented by E-mail, voice mail	Video programs supplemented by E-mail, videomessaging	Audio or video programs supplemented by voice mail or video messaging	Multimedia messaging
Two-way synchronous ("real time")	Phone, audio-conferencing	Telecollaboration, Internet	Interactive visual distance learning (IVDL), two-way video	Audiographics, personal computer application sharing, tele-collaboration	Video programs supplemented by telecollaboration	Audio or video programs supplemented by audioconferencing or IVDL	Interactive multimedia telecollaboration

FIGURE 2-1. Multiple media technology options.

tions, and these approaches are what we recommend to our clients in consulting engagements. Just as we use multiple transport systems to move people—airplanes, trains, automobiles—we need to use multiple media to move ideas in any form—audio, data, or video. The choice of technology and the mode of interaction—one-way, two-way asynchronous (delayed time), or two-way synchronous (real time)—depend on the needs of the organization and the design requirements for the distance learning program.

There is no one "best" technology. Each technology has different characteristics—strengths and limitations—that make it more or less appropriate for a given learning need. There are many ways to categorize technologies. One way is to sort them into groups based on the kind of message that is sent: audio, data (i.e., from a computer), video, or multimedia. Another way is to focus on the type of interaction made possible by the technology: one-way synchronous (real time), two-way synchronous, or two-way asynchronous (delayed time). This chapter and Chap. 3 give examples of the ways in which some of the more common technology options are used for distance learning today. Subsequent chapters discuss how one can choose the most appropriate technology or combinations of technologies for a specific learning objective, audience, or distance learning situation.

AUDIO TECHNOLOGIES: INEXPENSIVE ALTERNATIVES

Perhaps the simplest interactive distance learning technology option is the audio-only system based on the telephone. Telephone technologies have a number of advantages for distance education and training: They are readily available, they are familiar to users, they are reliable, and they are cost-effective.

The telephone is one of the most common pieces of office equipment. Although learning over the telephone, or educational audioconferencing, initially may seem to be a strange concept, consider the ways in which you and your coworkers are already using this technology for informal learning—for information exchange, problem solving, and decision making, for example. By expanding on the idea of the conference call by more formally integrating elements of course design, content, and delivery, instructors can use audioconferencing for the interactive delivery of training, to provide access to distant experts, and for ongoing professional collaboration and development.

Some instructors and students worry about the lack of a visual channel for communication in audio teleconferencing. However, research has shown that this form of delivery is effective for a variety of educational functions. Many experts emphasize that in most types of communication, including educational communications, audio is the most important channel of interaction. When visual input is needed to clarify, illustrate, or expand on audio communication, a visual channel can be added, sometimes through print materials and sometimes through the integration of an additional communications technology. By contrast, the arbitrary incorporation of video input that is not necessary for a particular subject matter or student population can be counterproductive. Educational research suggests that unnecessary visual input can be a distraction that causes cognitive overload and lowers achievement.

One of the most appealing benefits of audioconferencing is its cost-effectiveness. As is discussed below, the equipment needs—and therefore the costs—for training that uses telephone technologies can vary with the particular training situation. The type of equipment used also depends on the available resources and budget considerations. However, it is important to realize that the success of audioconference instruction is largely dependent on sound quality. While students are often willing and able to do without an interactive video channel, they won't put up with poor-quality audio. For this reason it is a good idea to invest in high-quality audioconferencing equipment, which can range in price from $150 to $2000 per unit (see Appendix B for a list of vendors that provide audioconferencing units). Remember, however, that the costs of even high-quality audioconferencing equipment and the associated telephone line charges are low compared with those of face-to-face training that requires students or instructors to travel.

The devices used for audioconferencing range from individual telephones and inexpensive speakerphones to specially designed systems that include speakers, microphones, and equipment to mix the sound. Although inexpensive speakerphones are sufficient when training is delivered to only a few students at a particular site or when the instruction periods are relatively short, for larger groups and/or longer instructional periods there may be a need for higher-quality equipment that typically employs digital signal processors (DSPs) that have echo cancellation circuits and noise control circuits that automatically adjust the unit to screen out ambient room noise. Whether the equipment used is simple or complex, the concept is simple: An instructor and students at multiple sites "meet" and interact in real time. This real-time conversational interaction is what makes audioconferencing so effective.

The familiarity and reliability of telephone technology minimize the need for technical support; because the training system is based on low-end technology, in most cases the instructor can operate the equipment without assistance. The usual dependability of telephone equipment does not eliminate the need for thorough testing and backup procedures, however. Someone—the instructor or a technical assistant—has to conduct preliminary tests of audio quality. These tests, particularly of the quality of intersite interactions, should be conducted far enough ahead of the classes to allow for the replacement or repair of equipment. Additionally, procedures for the restoration of temporarily disrupted telephone service or the replacement of a piece of equipment that fails unexpectedly should be developed and in place.

CASE STUDY: AUDIO TELECONFERENCING[1]

Often the technology that serves a client's needs best is not the most advanced or "high-tech." A good example is the Wisconsin Educational Teleconference Network (ETN), which since 1965 has provided continuing education via audioconferencing to physicians, allied health professionals, librarians, teachers, and other professionals in both rural and urban areas of that state. A companion audio service, WisLine, uses a conferencing bridge for state and university administrative meetings as well as continuing education.

Thirty years ago the University of Wisconsin wanted to find a way to provide educational access to professionals in that state, initially physicians, who needed to continue or update their education or training but were unable to travel to a remote campus. The search for a solution that would meet the diverse needs of residents throughout the state led to the development of the statewide audioconferencing system, ETN.

Although many powerful distance learning technologies have been developed during the last 30 years, audioconferencing remains the technology of choice for this network. The telephone network solution initially was chosen because of its two-way interactivity, ease of access, and cost-effectiveness. The early success of the continuing education programs for physicians resulted in strong support by the medical community and attracted the notice of other professional groups that needed to find an educational delivery system that would serve their needs. The ETN's willingness to focus on student needs, provide strong student support through the use of on-site coordinators, and continue to improve the technological aspects of the delivery system has ensured its success over the years. Enthusiastic support from clients, the University of Wisconsin system, and state agency partners have resulted in increasingly high levels of use: the ETN distance learning system now provides over 1700 hours of instruction annually, and WisLine is used more than 7400 hours per year.

AUDIO PLUS DATA TECHNOLOGIES: AUDIOGRAPHICS

Combining the audio capabilities of the telephone and the data capabilities of the computer creates a distance learning application called *audiographics.* In this learning environment, the telephone is used for two-way voice interaction and the computer is used to share graphic materials and allow collaborative work.

With an audiographic system, students can audioconference and see visual presentations at the same time. Students at different sites not only can view the same image simultaneously, they also can write or type messages that can be seen by all the members of the group. Some audiographic systems allow students to simultaneously share computer programs. Students at different sites can enter data into the same spreadsheet, producing a collaborative work space that is available to the students at every site. In some systems a digitizing camera can be used to produce images of drawings, people, and displays.

The audiographic equipment at each site generally includes audioconferencing apparatus, a computer and software, a modem, and peripheral devices such as a mouse, a graphics tablet, a scanner, and a camera. Voice and data are transmitted over standard telephone lines. Although some audiographic systems combine the voice and computer signals on a single telephone line, others use one line for voice and another one for data. Applications using audiographics range from one-time product update sessions to semesterlong courses for ongoing collaborative professional development. The cost of an audiographic system, depending on the type and quality of equipment, can range from $500 to $50,000. Appendix B gives contact information for some providers of audiographic equipment.

CASE STUDY: AUDIOGRAPHICS[2]

For over 25 years the University of Illinois has used distance learning to reach students throughout that state. The university's audiographic system, the Visual Teleconference System (VTS), has been used to connect geographically dispersed students and faculty members for credit and noncredit, undergraduate and graduate courses from the Colleges of Agriculture, Applied Life Science, Education, Engineering, and Liberal Arts and Sciences and from the Graduate School of Library and Information Science and the School of Social Work.

The basic VTS system configuration includes a computer, a high-speed modem, a laser printer, a keyboard, and an electronic writing tablet; an enhanced system may include a document scanner and a video camera. This combination of equipment allows the simultaneous sharing of sound, sight, and data messages between sites and thus provides a robust foundation for the delivery of different types of content and for interpersonal interaction at a variety of cognitive and affective levels.

Faculty members who teach via VTS use creative ways to humanize their technologically delivered classes. Some schedule at least one face-to-face class during the semester so that the students can get acquainted with each other and the instructor. Others arrange for pictures to be taken at each site and circulate them among all the participants or encourage students who live near each other to meet for lunch in order to get to know each other.

Audiographic systems such as VTS allow course material to be organized and presented in a variety of ways. Depending on the content, instructors usually mix and match a number of on-line and off-line activities. On-line activities, which allow students at different sites to interact, include brainstorming, question-and-answer sessions, and panel presentations. Off-line activities allow students at each site to work together and establish a sense of shared purpose; these activities include small-group projects, discussion sessions, and buzz groups.

Instructors who have used the system are enthusiastic about its ability to deliver the resources of the university to students who might otherwise be denied access to educational opportunities. They predict that the ability of VTS to expand access will increase with technological improvements and system enhancements.

AUDIO SUPPORT TECHNOLOGIES

Several audio communications support technologies, although neither powerful nor flexible enough to serve as primary delivery media, are widely used to support other forms of distance learning. These technologies include callback devices, voice mail, and facsimile (fax).

- *Callback devices.* Telephone technologies often are combined with one-way video systems to provide necessary or desired interactivity. Callback devices allow students receiving training via one-way video technologies such as satellite transmission to call the originating location to answer questions posed by the instructor, request feedback or clarification, and interact with other students.

- *Voice mail.* Voice mail allows telephone callers to leave a message that can be retrieved by the recipient at a later time. Voice mail also can be used as an effective teaching and learning tool, particularly when it is combined with other delivery technologies. Examples of the innovative use of voice mail include asynchronous student-instructor communications, feedback on or questions about assignments, and interim updates on course materials or procedures.

- *Fax.* Facsimile, or fax, machines allow the exchange of written or graphic information between geographically separated sites. Especially in cases where the main delivery system is audio-only, fax transmissions make the teaching-learning interaction more robust by supplementing audio interactions with visual information transmitted over telephone lines. Students or trainees can use fax machines to submit homework or project assignments.

VIDEO TECHNOLOGIES

Today distance learning uses a continuum of video communications technologies to integrate a vast array of instructional resources into a learning solution. Different types of video communications are being combined to mediate the flow of information among the organization, the instructors, and the students.

VIDEOTAPES

For over 20 years videotapes have been useful tools for management communications and training dissemination. An inexpensive videotape can capture an organizational leader's directives or a subject matter expert's message and make it available to others at a time and place convenient for them. A videotape of a respected organization leader also ensures that critical management communication is delivered in an effective and consistent manner throughout the enterprise.

Videotapes also can be used to provide cost-effective self-paced instruction and training for a variety of skills. For workers in the automotive industry, for example, the NAPA Institute of Automotive Technology (NIAT) offers independent study courses that include a videotape, a workbook (a pretest, quizzes, and shop exercises), and a final examination, which is mailed to NAPA for scoring. The 5 basic and 12 advanced courses in this program, which have been taken by over 30,000 students, cost NAPA approximately $80,000 each to develop; the courses sell for $89.50 each.[3]

ONE-WAY VIDEO BROADCASTS

While the industrial use of videotapes began years ago in the training departments of large companies, today critical management communication more typically is delivered via live business video broadcasts to provide a quick, effective, and credible method of communicating management directives throughout the company. The term *business video* refers to the use of one-way satellite broadcasts of management communications and training programs throughout an enterprise. Industry estimates suggest that more than 70 percent of business video programs are distance learning programs. Often, to achieve broader dissemination of critical messages, videotapes of the live broadcasts are later made available to employees and training departments.

Management and employee communication studies have shown that video is one of the most persuasive employee communications methods, especially when the message is presented by a person who is well known and holds a position of leadership. Business television programs provide an opportunity to reach large audiences quickly and with a unique impact. Business video broadcasts and videotapes are effective media for publicizing people, products, services, and events. Instructors should be aware that the most important element is the value of the message, not the quality of the production. The message must have a unique aspect that will be interesting and useful to the target audience.

One-way video distance learning applications are characterized by the transmission of video signals in only one direction: from the instructor to the students. A common method of delivering the video broadcast is by satellite. The components of a satellite broadcast system include the origination site, the satellite uplink for transmission of the program to a satellite orbiting the earth, the satellite transponder that receives the earth signal and retransmits it back to the earth, satellite downlink equipment, and a site for people to view the program on standard television monitors.

The program originates from a station on the earth and is transmitted to the satellite, which is in geostationary orbit; this means that the satellite "hovers" over the earth at the equator at a distance of 22,500 miles. As the earth rotates, the satellite rotates with it, appearing to stay at the same point in the sky. The satellite receives the video signal from the origination station on one frequency and rebroadcasts it back to the earth on another frequency. For example, satellite programs originating at one site in North America can be received simultaneously anywhere in the United States, serving a geographically dispersed audience. The area covered by the broadcast signal is referred to as the "footprint" on the earth. An almost limitless number of sites in the footprint area can receive the program.

The satellite receiving antenna can be fixed or stationary. Inexpensive fixed antennas costing less than $500 are frequently used to receive satellite programs such as direct broadcast satellite (DBS) entertainment programming. Steerable satellite antennas can cost several thousand dollars; however, they permit the user to access even more programs by pointing the antenna at other satellites in the sky. Both fixed and steerable antennas must be connected to a device called a satellite receiver, which converts the satellite transmission to a video and audio signal that can be sent to a television monitor.

The origination site can cost over $100,000, and skilled engineers are needed to monitor and maintain the transmission facility. Most training organizations contract for satellite transmission services, since few organizations require 7×24 (seven days a week for 24 hours a day) use of a broadcast facility. Transponder use time can average $700 per hour for domestic satellites and $3000 per hour for an international program. It is advisable for the training organization to focus on the development and delivery of the training program content and contract with a network service provider for the transmission of the satellite video signal.

Many businesses combine one-way video transmission of training materials with the interactive capabilities of two-way data or audio communication. Ford, for example, uses the FORDSTAR Satellite Communications Network to broadcast hundreds of hours of training monthly to the company's technicians and salespeople. Instructors use a variety of technologies—including a computer for PowerPoint demonstrations, an overhead projector, a laser disc player, and a VCR—in addition to the satellite transmission to conduct their classes. Students at the receiving sites see and hear the instructor and his or her presentation on the television monitors and can respond to questions posed by the instructor by using electronic keypads. Other companies and institutions use audio bridges to combine two-way voice interaction with one-way satellite transmission.[4]

VIDEO ON DEMAND

Another video program service that has the potential to become a popular training dissemination vehicle is Video on Demand (VOD). VOD had its origins in test-marketing trials of a cable television service that enabled residential customers to access hundreds of movies from a terminal attached to their home television sets. The viewers selected a movie and used a telephone line to send the request to their cable operators, which in turn made the movie available on a particular channel. Customers did not have to travel to the local store to rent a videotape; instead, they selected from a menu of options and agreed to pay a fee for viewing a particular movie. The service has not been widely deployed in public cable networks but has enjoyed success in hotels and closed-circuit networks for years.

From a training point of view, VOD services allow the content of a video training program to be hosted in video servers on an organization's data network. In the future, with increases in the bandwidth available for public networks, video training programs could be hosted on Internet servers and made available to anyone with high-speed data access and a multimedia personal computer (PC).

VIDEO PLUS CBT

Video program content can be supplemented with other training technology to create a powerful communications pattern. Video, computer-based training (CBT), and data resources can enable learners to experience a variety of training delivery media as they complete units of instruction. In CBT (discussed more fully below) the computer is the instrument of learning. Many forms of CBT exist, including computer-assisted instruction (CAI), computer-assisted learning (CAL), and computer-managed instruction (CMI). CAI and CAL provide drill and practice, tutorials, simulations, and games. CMI can perform routine data-processing tasks that are useful to instructors, such as assessing students, revising materials, and testing. Multimedia CBT programming incorporates text, graphics, audio, video, and data in the delivery of the training content.

Much of the discussion of video technology options up to this point has focused on the one-way presentation of training materials. CBT goes a step beyond these one-way technologies by providing an element of interaction. However, it is interaction only in a highly structured, preprogrammed sense. (CBT is discussed further later in this chapter.)

TWO-WAY VIDEO

A two-way video distance learning system provides video and audio communications in both directions between learners and instructors. All the locations in a two-way video system are equipped with cameras, monitors, and microphones. Point-to-point and multipoint connections enable instructors and learners to see and hear each other.

The ability of students to see and hear an instructor brings new levels of interaction to the distance learning experience. Problem solving, demonstration, behavior modeling, and skills practice are all enhanced by the addition of two-way video. Distance learning applications using two-way video technology fall into two general categories: compressed video and full-motion video.

Compressed Video.   Compressed video systems offer the flexibility of a variety of bandwidth services to the user. The audio and video signals go through digital signal processing that eliminates redundant information, thereby reducing the bandwidth necessary to transmit information between locations. The compressed signals can be sent to virtually any location over the switched telephone network. When switched digital services are used, the quality of the picture is a function of how much bandwidth is used. The cost of the connection is based on the bandwidth used.

Full-Motion Video. A full-motion video distance learning system provides picture quality that is comparable to that of commercial television. These systems typically require an investment in fiber-optic cables, high-capacity circuits, and Asychronous Transfer Mode (ATM) or satellite transponder access to link learning sites together. Full-motion network systems often are built with private full-time or part-time transmission paths to support them.

The selection of a video system is influenced by learning requirements and cost factors. The technology is changing rapidly, and the trend is toward better-quality video and audio on less expensive worldwide transport services.

CASE STUDY: VIDEO TELECONFERENCING[5]

United Technologies Corporation (UTC), an international company with over 168,000 employees, produces a wide range of products and services for the aerospace, building, and automotive industries. Annual revenues from these high-technology products amount to over $21 billion, and professional training and development is a high priority, especially for the company's scientists and engineers. In the rapidly changing field of advanced technologies, technical knowledge and skills can become obsolete quickly. UTC needed an effective and efficient way to maintain professional competencies while providing training in emerging technologies that are important to its operations and customers.

The design and delivery of technical education and training to the company's community of professional engineers and scientists have traditionally been carried out by the Technical Training and Education Department and through a program that delivers information from leading universities to engineers and scientists at company locations around the world. Recently, UTC began looking for ways to expand and enhance this industry-university collaboration.

The company first investigated different ways to meet the educational needs of UTC professionals: having students enroll in courses at local universities, bringing instructors to UTC, building in-house corporate universities, videotaping and distributing broadcasts, and using interactive compressed video (ICV) technology. After study, ICV was chosen as the best way to bring world-class technical training from Boston University (BU) to UTC's global workplace.

Beginning in 1991, a BU professor delivered a semesterlong graduate engineering course via interactive videoconferencing from Boston to students at a UTC division (Hamilton Standard) in Windsor Locks, Connecticut. In the next semester graduate courses were delivered to three UTC divisions in Connecticut and Maine. Bridging services that supported multipoint videoconferencing were used to ensure an effective virtual classroom environment despite the inclusion of additional sites.

During the first year and a half of the program's operation, almost 25,000 hours of education was delivered. Today, all the divisions of UTC receive graduate-level engineering courses and/or specialized technical and certificate programs courses, and/or short courses and seminars via ICV. During the course of the project, the number of educational providers expanded to include Boston University, Penn State, the Hartford Graduate Center, the University of Maryland, the University of Connecticut, Georgia Tech, Rensselaer Polytechnical Institute, Massachusetts Institute of Technology, Columbia University, and Stanford University.

One of the major benefits to students is the extent to which ICV supports interaction between students and instructors and among students. This characteristic allows students to ask for immediate clarification or provide timely input on a course topic, a feature lacking in some other forms of distance learning, such as one-way satellite broadcasts and videotaped presentations. Especially in dealing with complex subject matter, interactivity can facilitate and enhance learning. Other benefits include considerable reductions in travel and labor costs and the realization of economies of scale through the use of services such as multipoint bridging.

A comprehensive approach to distance learning applications takes all the technology options into consideration and builds systems that include many of the technologies mentioned here. A variety of combinations are in use today; an example would be a two-way video system that uses fax and Internet E-mail communications for student assignments and additional student-to-instructor and student-to-student interaction. Solutions such as video teleconferencing, multipoint conferencing student response systems, and Internet-based collaborative learning (all of which are discussed in detail later in this chapter and in Chap. 3) are providing educators and trainers with new and more powerful tools to reach and engage their learners.

COMPUTER-BASED TRAINING

Computer-based training is a training delivery mode in which a computer is used as a tool to deliver and/or manage learning experiences. The two major forms of CBT are computer-assisted instruction and computer-managed instruction.

CAI focuses on the delivery of instruction by using the computer as the delivery mechanism. CAI is well suited for learning experiences that require drill and practice, tutorials, simulations, and instructional games. The student reads information presented on the screen and interacts with the content by using a mouse or keyboard. The student controls the pace of the instruction, and the computer controls the sequence of steps through the learning experience.

In CMI, the computer automates the routine data-tracking and information-processing tasks instructors perform: registering, testing, and mentoring students and keeping student records. CMI also may be used to diagnose the learning needs of individual students and prescribe optimal sequences of instruction. CMI enables the instructor to manage the provision of individualized instruction to many students.

Control Data Corporation was one of the early pioneers in providing CBT services to corporate clients. Its product, PLATO (Programmed Logic for Automated Teaching Operations), was initially developed in 1960 at the University of Illinois. The PLATO system was deployed in over a thousand corporate, higher education, and government sites throughout the world. Terminals with modems connected the students by telephone lines to the PLATO mainframe computer, which held hundreds of course titles, tutorials, drills and practice modules, and tests. PLATO employed hierarchical programmed instruction with both linear and branching capabilities. Early terminals had the ability to present only text and simple monochrome graphics to the students; even so, significant learning gains and time reduction for learning mastery were reported for CBT programs.

With the advent of microcomputers and minicomputers in the late 1970s and the PC in the early 1980s, CBT began to move away from the terminal and mainframe environments toward stand-alone, desktop computer environments. Processing power increased dramatically, graphics and text capabilities improved, color and sound were added, and the widespread availability and affordability of local Random Access Memory (RAM) and mass storage memory devices made stand-alone desktop computers the preferred way to deliver CBT. Also, hundreds of authoring programs and approaches for delivering CBT were developed.

CBT can be useful to companies that want to provide self-paced independent training. The automotive company Bear, for example, offers courses in electronic fuel injection and wheel alignment in this format. The computer disks for each course include a pretest, an introduction to the topic, a discussion of diagnostic procedures and troubleshooting, and a posttest.[6]

NOTES

1. This case study was summarized from "Educational Teleconference Network (ETN) and WisLine," one of the on-line case studies of Lucent Technologies' Center for Excellence in Distance Learning (http://www.lucent.com/cedl/wisline.htm).

2. Summarized from F. Mastny, T. Shuttle, A. Wadsworth, and S. Hsu. 1995. Audiographics reaches students at remote sites extramural programs. *ETAG Newsletter* (July–August) (http://www.oir.uiuc.edu/etag/newsletr/exmural/mastny/mastny.html).

3. Weber, B. 1997. Going the distance for learning. *Motor Age Online* (February) (http://www.motorage.com/edindex/029718.htm).

4. Organization for Economic Cooperation and Development. 1996. OECD Proceedings. *Adult learning in a new technological era.* Paris: OECD Publications.

5. Summarized from Biegleck, S. Corporate distance learning: Global business video services (http://www.lucent.com/cedl/utc.html).

6. Weber, 1997.

ADVANCED COMPUTER TECHNOLOGIES

COMPUTER CONFERENCING, ELECTRONIC PERFORMANCE SUPPORT SYSTEMS, THE INTERNET, AND THE WORLD WIDE WEB

COMPUTER CONFERENCING

Computer conferencing is a general term that includes several distinct but related activities in which computers support and facilitate communication between people. The three most common forms of computer-based conferencing are electronic mail (E-mail), group conferencing systems, and interactive messaging systems. All these systems can be used effectively in educational and training applications.

E-MAIL

The simplest form of E-mail involves one-to-one communication between two computer users. The originator of the message types it on his or her computer and special software directs the computer to send it electronically (via the telephone lines) to another user, who can choose to read it, download it, discard it, store it, or forward it. One way to extend the distribution of the message is by typing in the names and computer addresses of multiple recipients. However, many enhanced E-mail systems automate this function by creating and managing a distribution list for messages.

Enhanced E-mail "exploder" systems such as Listserv have both a management function and a distribution function. First, they manage the list of subscribers or group members, which can number in the thousands, by keeping track of those who join (sign on) and those who resign from (sign off) the conferencing group. Second, they copy any message contributed by an individual and distribute it to all the group members. The system also stores or "archives" a copy of each message. In this way new subscribers can recall and read previous interactions to understand the background and prior discussion of a topic.

In education or training applications, electronic mail, like voice mail, allows students to leave questions for instructors which can be answered at a later time. However, E-mail is more powerful than voice mail because the question-and-answer exchanges can be stored for other students to see; in this way, the same questions are not answered again and again over the duration of a course.

Any distance learning system can be made more student-centered by improving the quality and in some cases the quantity of the interactions between the instructor and the students and those among the students. Many students have reported being pleasantly surprised to find that they have more interactions and opportunities for interaction in a distance learning environment than they would in many face-to-face classes. Busy working professionals who have little time for formal learning during the business day find that E-mail allows them to have ongoing interaction with fellow professionals throughout the course of study.

Using E-mail for instructional interactions has many other benefits. A major benefit for the student is that he or she determines the time and place of an interaction. The student has an opportunity to reflect on a question and provide a well-thought-out response. For this reason, many students prefer the less threatening E-mail responses to the thinking-on-your-feet responses required in a face-to-face classroom setting.

Many training organizations with global responsibilities are finding not only that E-mail interaction makes distance learning across multiple time zones and cultures easier but also that it is the preferred medium of expression for students who speak English as a second language. Those students are often overwhelmed in rapid question-and-answer sessions in a traditional classroom setting. Also, it may be culturally difficult or even inappropriate for them to question or challenge an instructor in a face-to-face setting. The time delay of the interactions in E-mail communication makes it possible for international students to be more reflective and word their comments carefully in responding to discussion topics or posing questions. The time delay also gives an analytic student the opportunity to research information before being required to respond.

As was mentioned earlier, most E-mail systems automatically keep a record of these interactions, which can be sorted by respondent, date, and sometimes topic. The storing, or archiving, of previous messages adds to the power and flexibility of this medium. A student can join a discussion late and still have the feeling of being a participant in the thought process that led to the development of the ideas. Similarly, E-mail discussions can easily be embellished by "bringing in" outside subject matter experts who can add their knowledge to the educational discourse that has developed through the extended exchange of messages; this supplemental dialogue then becomes part of the permanent record of the class.

GROUP CONFERENCING SYSTEMS

In general, group conferencing systems extend the features and functions of electronic mail. These systems are designed to handle the needs that arise when interaction extends beyond two participants. In other words, whereas E-mail is often a one-to-one activity, group conferencing is a one-to-many or many-to-many activity. Group conferencing systems are used to manage the functions involved in group-oriented computer-based interactions. These functions include the management of group membership lists, the efficient distribution of messages to group members, and the storage and retrieval of prior interactions. Two types of group conferencing systems are the bulletin board system and the conference management system.

A bulletin board system (BBS) provides the function that its name implies: It is a place to "post" messages of interest to the community that sponsors and maintains the system. Just as is the case with a real-world bulletin board, a "virtual" bulletin board often is divided into sections based on the content of the message. Users can send, or post, messages to the appropriate area of the bulletin board; other users can reply directly to the sender of a message or distribute their responses to all the members of the conferencing group.

Conference management systems provide a structured approach to group conferences. They use database management features that allow the establishment of an asynchronous discussion forum through "threaded discussions," or discussions in which responses to questions and comments are visually organized in a hierarchy, making it easy to follow a line of reasoning—a thread. As the asynchronous discussions grow, the responses typically are placed in chronological order under topic headings. Sophisticated group conferencing systems permit students to search messages for key words and sort responses by specified characteristics. These functions are particularly useful when the topics of messages are diverse and wide-ranging and/or when the number of group members is very large.

The structured approach of conference management systems makes them easy to learn and use and particularly valuable in supporting instructional communication. In instructional settings students can interact with their instructors, with outside content experts, and among themselves in both task-oriented and more informal exchanges. In this way, group computer conferencing fosters "many-to-many" communication.

Professor Roger Caldwell at the University of Arizona teaches a course on the impact of future technologies on the economy and society. He asks his students to interact freely through E-mail dialogue not only with the instructors but with other students as well. He poses thought-provoking questions that serve as catalysts for threaded E-mail discussions and also involves two or three subject matter experts each semester to give the course additional depth and richness.

Subject matter experts volunteer to participate because they know that they will have the ability to control the amount of interaction as well as the time and place of interaction. From the subject matter expert's point of view, such discussion opportunities provide a chance to test their theories and ideas with groups of students—often practicing professionals—different from the audiences with which they typically interact.

Increasingly, universities are using conference management systems to support distance learning programs. Examples of conference management systems used for this purpose include VAXNotes, CoSy, Confer, and FirstClass.

INTERACTIVE MESSAGING SYSTEMS

While most computer conferencing is asynchronous, or time-delayed, some conferencing systems support synchronous, or real-time, communication. In interactive messaging, a person types a message on his or her computer screen and the message appears simultaneously on the screens of all the other members of the group. The messaging system automatically appends the name of the sender of each message and manages the flow of messages. This type of conferencing interaction is useful when feedback is needed quickly or when a discussion will benefit from a more natural flow, as in brainstorming sessions. Examples of messaging systems are the UNIX "Talk" program and the Internet Relay Chat (IRC) system.

GROUPWARE

A specialized conferencing application, groupware, combines delayed and real-time communication features in a way that makes it particularly useful in business environments. Groupware creates an "electronic work space" that supports a variety of functions. For example, based on the conferencing concept described above, groupware can sort, organize, and store the inputs of group participants as well as support group processes such as idea generation, evaluation, and consensus building. It also allows for data sharing and collaboration among a group of networked (that is, connected through their computers) users. Group members can simultaneously work on the same document or spreadsheet, and any changes made appear immediately on each individual's computer screen. Some groupware programs have other specialized features, including automatic organization of a group's telephone messages, appointments, facility schedules, memos, and work assignments. Examples of groupware programs include IBM's Person-to-Person and Novell's Groupwise.

ELECTRONIC PERFORMANCE
SUPPORT SYSTEMS

Electronic performance support systems (EPSSs) provide integrated, on-demand access to information, knowledge, and tools that enable the user to perform his or her job with minimal support from others and/or minimal training. The goal of a performance support system is to accelerate the user through the learning curve to improved job performance. Performance support tools provide whatever is necessary to generate performance and learning at the moment of need. They enable novice users to perform at an acceptable level the first day on the job. EPSSs typically are made up of one or all of the following components: tools, knowledge bases, expert system advisers, and learning experiences.

The tool component of an EPSS is designed to increase productivity in the use of application software. The templates that are included in Microsoft products are examples of performance support tools. The "spell check" function that is included in most word processing packages and the formula creation function included in most spreadsheet functions are other examples.

Knowledge bases typically include information stored in a hyperlink format that is easily accessed when needed by the user. Policy and procedure manuals are examples of the type of information most often converted to hyperlinked performance support knowledge bases. Product information, regulatory guidelines, and technical specifications are other examples. Some of the more innovative performance support knowledge bases incorporate *agent technology*, which remembers the content areas an individual accesses most often and informs that individual of any new information that has been added since the last time he or she accessed the information.

"Expert system advisers" are interactive, context-sensitive reasoning systems designed to "coach" an individual through the process of performing procedures and making decisions. Turbo Tax, a popular tax preparation software package, guides users through the process of completing income tax returns. Turbo Tax "interviews" the user as a tax consultant would, provides tax law information, and guides the user in completing his or her return. When the return is completed, Turbo Tax runs a check on the return and advises the user of areas that could be audited.

The learning experience component of a performance support system is similar to that of traditional computer-based training (CBT); the primary difference lies in the design of the content. Learning experiences are designed to provide information, examples, practice, and feedback in small chunks, typically taking less than 5 minutes and not more than 10 minutes to complete. The learning experience is usually context-linked to other components of the performance support system. For example, if a user is in the middle of an interview with the expert system adviser and does not understand the questions being asked or the response required, he or she accesses the learning component of the performance system and obtains the instructions required to proceed.

DESIGN OF A PERFORMANCE SUPPORT SYSTEM

Because the primary goal of a performance support system is to support users in the performance of their jobs, we recommend that the processes of the organization drive the design of the EPSS. Electronic performance support systems designed in this manner are more closely related to the individual's job and thus provide a greater transferable benefit. To illustrate this point, we discuss below how a performance support tool was developed to support the claims settlement process of a major property and casualty (P&C) insurance company.

The P&C company's business strategy was that of operational excellence. This strategy requires that a company rely on efficient transactions to improve productivity and ensure high-quality customer service. By documenting the claims process and structuring its performance support system around the process, the company was able to achieve gains in both productivity and level of service (Fig. 3-1).

It is during the "investigative" phase of the claims process that a claims representative must verify coverage, gather facts concerning the loss, and analyze those facts. By selecting "Investigative Phase" on the process map, the claims representative is presented with different options. One option is to obtain an explanation of what is expected during this phase (Fig. 3-2).

If the claims representative requires more information about the investigative phase, he or she may access a brief cased-based tutorial that provides a practical example, practice, and feedback related to investigating a claim.

During the investigative stage the claims representative also may have questions related to vehicle recall information from the manufacturer or the National Highway and Traffic Safety Administration. The claims representative has the option to access the EPSS knowledge base and go to the National Highway and Traffic Safety Administration's Web site to see whether the vehicle under investigation has been recalled.

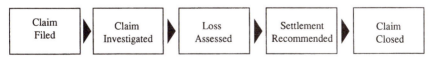

FIGURE 3-1.   Claims process.

EXPLANATION OF THE INVESTIGATIVE PHASE

The second phase in settling a claim is to investigate the circumstances related to the claim, the coverage of the claimant, and the policy. You need to determine whether you have enough information to verify that the vehicle is a covered automobile and the coverages on the claim are correct. There are four steps in claims investigation:

1. Collecting information related to policy and coverage
2. Analyzing the policy and coverage
3. Collecting information related to the loss
4. Analyzing the loss-related information

    During the course of your investigation you may identify indicators of potential fraud. Remember that these are only indicators. The fraud investigation unit should do any further investigation into the possibility of a fraudulent claim.

FIGURE 3-2.   Explanation of the investigative phase.

    As the claims representative begins the analysis of the coverage, he or she may access the Coverage Analysis Checklist from the tools portion of the performance support tool (Fig. 3-3). The checklist recommends the steps and considerations the claims representative must take into account in analyzing the coverage. Because insurance policies may vary by state, the claims representative also may choose to review the policy by going into the knowledge base and accessing the policy that covers the vehicle.

    An additional component of the performance support system is an idea section where claims representatives can access and post the suggestions and findings acquired from their personal experiences. This type of application supports organizational learning and builds on the intellectual capital of the organization.

    In the claims settlement example, we illustrated how a performance support tool designed to support a business process can be easily accessed to support specific tasks related to the performance of a job. Again, the primary goal of performance support is to enable

COVERAGE ANALYSIS CHECKLIST

To analyze coverage you must verify policy information to make sure the policyholder has the proper coverage for the loss. Use this checklist to verify that the proper coverage exists:

1. Verify that coverage exists.
2. Compare the coverage(s) opened with the coverage(s) in force.
3. Verify the deductible amount.
4. Compare the name of the driver with the persons insured in the policy.
5. Compare the reported vehicle with the vehicles listed in the policy.
6. Verify the use and location of the vehicle at the time of the accident or loss. Some uses and locations are excluded in the auto policy.
7. Communicate your decision promptly.

FIGURE 3-3.   Coverage analysis checklist.

an individual to perform his or her job at the time of need with as little time away from the job as possible.

DEVELOPMENT OF PERFORMANCE SUPPORT TOOLS

The composition of the development team for creating an EPSS is similar to that for other distance learning applications. The simplest team is composed of a designer-developer who is familiar with performance system development, content experts who are expert performers, and a technical-system expert who can creatively represent the content electronically. If video and graphics are part of the performance support system, it is necessary to include someone with expertise in those areas.

The content should be organized around the process that is being supported. There are several different ways to design and organize content. Some methods are grounded in cognitive psychology theories and can be very complex and time-consuming to develop.

We have found that the simplest method for structuring the content for an EPSS is to ask three basic questions: What does the person need to know? What does the person need to do? and What does the person need to have? Because these questions ask for information within the context of performing the job, they are relatively easy for content experts to answer.

In the claims example above, the claims representative needed to know what was involved in the investigative phase of a claim. The performance support system supplied the representative with a process map and an explanation. In the investigative phase the claims representative needed to analyze the coverages included in the policy. The performance system supplied the representative with a checklist for analyzing the policy. Finally, the claims representative needed to have access to the policy, and the policy was included in the support knowledge base.

The tool used to develop the performance support system varies with the requirements for supporting job performance. Performance support tools such as checklists, cue cards, and explanations can be developed with any one of a number of commercial tools that support the creation of automated help. Performance support tools such as "coaches" and "guides" can be developed by using off-the-shelf CBT development software. The selection of a development tool should be based on the applications requirements.

How you distribute your performance support system is dependent on how and where your user will need access to it (Table 3-1).

TABLE 3-1. **Means of Distributing an EPSS**

LOCATION	ADVANTAGES	DISADVANTAGES
Hard drive	• Quicker access • Easier to integrate into work flow	• Difficult to update • Limited availability of space on hard drive
CD-ROM	• Stores large volumes of information	• Difficult to update • Dependent on availability of CD-ROM drives
LAN	• Easiest medium to keep updated	• Must have telecommunications access

The most common means of distributing an EPSS are the hard drive of the workstation, CD-ROM, and a local area network (LAN).

Electronic performance support systems are designed to affect performance directly and immediately. In their attempt to eliminate the distinction between learning and work, they have transformed the worker and the work environment. By reducing the learning curve, electronic performance support tools enable workers to be productive the first day on the job.

EDUCATION AND TRAINING ON THE INTERNET

One of the chief challenges in training and education today is to find ways to quickly disseminate new policy information, product information, and service-related information to a widely dispersed audience. One cannot rely on traditional channels for the dissemination of information. In the traditional training environment people often had to wait for months, maybe as long as a year, to get into a required training course. These delays resulted from a shortage of qualified instructors or training facilities and from the personal scheduling conflicts of busy students.

In today's business environment, change is a constant. There is a need to create within organizations continuous learning environments that allow employees to easily access the learning resources they need to keep informed about the changes that are occurring in their companies and professions. The Internet offers a basis for the creation of flexible learning environments that meet many of the educational and training needs of organizations in today's information society.

THE NEED FOR FLEXIBLE, CONTINUOUS LEARNING ENVIRONMENTS

Knowledge workers today are constantly confronted with new products and services, policies and procedures, and price structures. These types of changes used to run in 12- to 24-month planning cycles; today, however, significant changes occur almost on a monthly basis. This phenomenon is especially apparent in the Web software business, where the Web "year" has shrunk to about three months. These changes in business and industry are causing people to develop new ways to bring geographically dispersed employees up to date quickly.

Hewlett-Packard reports that the half-life of a software engineer's knowledge is on the order of 2½ years: After 2½ years, half of what the engineer learned in his or her initial training has become obsolete. Without continuously updated training, these engineers can no longer bring the same value to the organization that they did the day they were hired from college. The rapid rate of technological development also means that much of the information a fourth-year software engineering student learned in his or her freshman and sophomore years is obsolete upon graduation. There is a need for mechanisms for continuous training and retraining to keep these professionals knowledgeable in their fields.

The need for perpetual changes in curricula may not be as dramatic in some fields as it is in software engineering, but most knowledge workers share a need for continuous training to remain proficient in their jobs. This training is necessary not only for people in technical areas but also for those in sales, service, manufacturing, and human resources. The entire organization needs to remain current so that it can remain competitive.

Corporate executives understand that training and retraining are critical to the success of an organization. However, they also need to understand that changing conditions often necessitate changing training strategies. While face-to-face instruction worked well for many years, it cannot accommodate all of today's training challenges. The rate of change of information and time-to-market pressures dictate the embrace of new delivery systems that can reach large, geographically dispersed audiences in cost-effective, time-efficient ways. In many cases Internet-based distance learning technologies offer the needed solutions.

THE INTERNET

The Internet is a network of networks. What does that mean? We like to explain what the Internet does for data communications by comparing it to what the worldwide public telephone network does for voice communications. Virtually anyone with a telephone can connect with anyone else. Even though different states, regions, and countries have different telephone companies and may have different types of equipment, there are well-established rules and protocols that make it possible for a person to talk from his or her home to someone on the other side of the globe. If you have the right equipment, have access to a local telephone company, and know the distant telephone number, you can be connected.

The Internet is in many ways similar. To send and receive data communications you need the right equipment and software, you need an access point to the Internet, and you have to know the unique address of the distant personal computer or server you are trying to reach. Most people are not as interested in how telephone or data communications systems work as they are in effectively using those systems. However, we will provide a brief technical explanation that offers some insights into a few of the challenges that distance learning practitioners face (and overcome) when they use the Internet to deliver training programs.

The Internet was established in the 1970s as a packet network with multiple-path routing because the U.S. Department of Defense wanted to build networks that could withstand partial outages during national emergencies. The Defense Department created a network called ARPAnet and various other radio and satellite networks. The ARPAnet was a research experiment to see how information could be routed through the Internet using the Internet Protocol (IP).

THE WORLD WIDE WEB

The World Wide Web (WWW) is a facet of the Internet consisting of client and server computers that store multimedia documents. The WWW is a project that began at the Conseil Européen pour la Recherdie Nucléaire (CERN), the European particle physics laboratory. Its primary goal was to make it easier for physicists to collaborate by allowing them to share all types of information in real time. The WWW uses a client-server model with information "hosted," or stored, on networked servers accessed by personal computer (PC) clients. The WWW might have remained a CERN project if Tim Berners-Lee, the WWW's project leader, had not made the specifications public. Soon the WWW began to find new communities of users and information providers. The client computers use software packages called *browsers* to view multimedia documents, and the server computers use server software to maintain documents for clients to access.

Web Documents.   Web documents are created by using a standard language called Hyper Text Markup Language (HTML), which uses short codes called tags to designate graphic elements and links. Clicking on a link brings the documents on the server to a PC's browser. The documents may contain text, images, sounds, movies, or a combination of multimedia elements. Another commonly used

Internet term is MIME, which stands for multipurpose Internet mail extension. This is a standardized method for organizing divergent file formats in which the MIME type establishes whether a file format can be read by the browser software's built-in capabilities or whether a suitable helper application is available to read a file.

Documents are addressed with a uniform resource locator (URL). A URL indicates where the content is located on a networked server; every Internet address has a URL which indicates an organizational affiliation. Browsers provide an easy-to-use "point and click" interface to the information on the WWW and make it possible to access documents. Following are some common URL suffixes and the organizational affiliations they represent: .com (commercial), .edu (educational), .gov (government), .mil (military), .net (networking), and .org (noncommercial). URLs from outside the United States often use a two-letter suffix that designates a country, for example, .uk (United Kingdom), .jp (Japan), .ca (Canada), and .nl (Netherlands).

Some companies maintain a link to the Internet through a dedicated communication line. Those which do not require a dedicated circuit to access the Internet through an Internet Service Provider (ISP). Most individuals access the Internet through ISPs. If you have a modem—generally with at least 14,400 bits per second (bps) speed—you dial the ISP and log on to a computer that is connected to the Internet. Today's Internet software and data networking technology make access to training programs virtually ubiquitous for anyone with a PC and a browser. Internet browsers such as Microsoft's Internet Explorer and Netscape's Navigator can be obtained free of charge. Students can obtain dial-up access to the Internet from their homes by subscribing to an ISP such as America on Line (AOL) for as little as $5 a month for five hours of service or $20 a month for an unlimited number of access hours.

Intranets and Extranets.   Many companies set up private Internets called intranets. Only employees and people with special access privileges can use these intranets. A "firewall" forms the boundary between the intranet's networked computers within the corporation and other computers connected to the Internet. This firewall protects one or more computers with Internet connection from being accessed by external computers. The PCs within the firewall are on a secure subnet with internal access capabilities and shared resources that are not available to PCs on the outside.

Many companies host their proprietary distance learning training programs on their intranets. If employees need to access the external Internet from the internal intranets, devices called *proxy servers* are used. Proxy servers give employees access to Internet resources from a PC connected within a firewall. Data networking technologies that provide other corporate computer services can be adapted to provide training programs on the same LANs or corporate wide area networks (WANs).

Another variation on the Internet is called an extranet, which often is established to allow people outside an organization who have Internet access to obtain some resources that may be considered proprietary. An extranet is a network that has IDs and passwords that allow an organization to control who accesses the information it hosts. For example, extranets are a useful way to provide distance learning training materials to preferred customers and distributors.

ADVANTAGES OF INTERNET-BASED AND WEB-BASED DELIVERY OF PROGRAMS

Internet-based delivery of training programs allows a corporation to avoid the cumbersome logistics of maintaining dedicated training facilities, which can be quite expensive. With Internet delivery, organizations can focus their limited resources on developing training programs, not on delivering training to the workplace.

The Internet is one of the most basic yet powerful options available to deliver and update training quickly. Today, there are a wide variety of Internet delivery options available to corporate trainers. The ease of use of common browsers makes them suitable for virtually anyone with PC skills. Update information can be hosted, and learners can read it, discuss it freely through real-time computer interaction in "chat" rooms, and question instructors with on-line discussions or electronic mail to obtain the clarification they need to be successful in a course. Groups of learners can participate in protracted conversations in cyberspace. Learners also can complete testing exercises on the Web to obtain certification. In fact, the entire learning transaction can be accommodated in the cyberspace environment.

Another advantage of Web-based delivery of content is that training developers can disseminate and update information immediately rather than worrying about having to change the training materials and mail out the changed materials to remote sites. The updates can be done electronically on the Web so that any student accessing the information after an update has been hosted receives the most current information. Also, students can use the updated Web content as a source of current reference materials on their jobs. For example, the AT&T Network Engineering and Operations Training Organization allows students who have completed a course on the Web to become alumni of that course. The alumni are given permanent IDs and passwords so that when they have questions about the course content, they can go back to the Web site and access the most current information. In contrast, if students participate in a face-to-face course, the information they take away in the course binder most likely will become obsolete soon after they complete the course.

CBT AND THE WORLD WIDE WEB

Some organizations are beginning to experiment with new and more powerful ways to combine other distance learning technologies with WWW delivery of training programs. Computer-based training approaches are especially appropriate for this type of synthesis. CBT programs can be downloaded from the Web and then run on a local PC just as if they were installed from a diskette or CD-ROM. Students who complete a CBT module may be directed to send E-mail comments to an instructor or other students, or they may be required to access the WWW to demonstrate their mastery of the content through the completion of an on-line test.

More sophisticated applications permit students to use the WWW and CBT on CD-ROM in combination. For example, a major manufacturer stores audio and motion video segments on a CD-ROM so that a student does not have to wait long for the large video files to be downloaded from the Web. The CD-ROM delivers a high-quality audio and video presentation on the desktop, and the WWW is used to access the most current technical information or update prices on the product. The student has the option of loading the most current information by activating a link to the WWW from within the CBT program. Other options for updating the CD-ROM content include loading all the new information before the CD-ROM program is run and loading all the updates after the training session on the CD-ROM has been completed. Some browsers permit application sharing so that students and instructors can simultaneously view the CBT program and collaboratively work their way through the content.

Innovation and change are constant in the world of CBT, and the WWW has introduced many new options for information sharing and collaboration. In the world of distance learning one can expect to see many more instructional technology hybrids that will enable instructors and students to create powerful customized learning experiences in a distance learning environment.

NETWORKED DISTANCE LEARNING ENVIRONMENTS

The technologies that are available today make it possible to create networked distance learning environments. It is now possible to put the learners at the center of the learning experience and surround them with a variety of rich information and knowledge resources. These resources include instructors-facilitators-mentors who are assigned to help individual students through a course.

These resources also include learner support services that are similar to the customer sales and service staffs that operate call centers or customer care centers today. A call center provides high-quality student services such as promoting course offerings, registration services, fulfillment services, and "hot line" support so that students' questions can be answered quickly.

Another component of the networked distance learning environment is access to a virtual library. A virtual library is similar to a library on campus where the instructor can put resources and recommended reading materials on reserve. Through the access capabilities of the Internet, the instructor can host update information; provide a set of Web "bookmarks," or direct links to resources; and then assign students to go out on the Internet to search for information that is relevant to the unit of study. An additional advantage of creating a virtual library is that when students access a valuable resource, they can create a bookmark of the URL for themselves. This resource is then held on their PCs as part of their personal virtual libraries, which they can retrieve whenever they need the information, often long after the end of a course.

ROLE OF THE INSTRUCTORS IN INTERNET LEARNING

The role of the instructor or faculty member is changing. Internet-based distance learning enables an instructor to take a much more learner-centered approach. Instead of delivering lectures and assuming or hoping that the same lecture will address the needs of a diverse group of students in the classroom, instructors can focus and deliver the content that is most relevant to individual students. The instructor becomes a synthesizer of information who can create unique learning experiences tailored to the individual needs of students. Instructors who do not use these new technologies may be shortchanging themselves and their organizations.

Will Distance Learning Make Instructors Obsolete?   Can technologies replace the need for a live instructor? The issue of technology replacing a live instructor has been debated at great length for many years. The debate on technology in education goes all the way back to the days of Gutenberg's invention of movable type for the printing press. Early professors thought that the widespread availability of books would eliminate the need for residential campuses, but that was not the case. In fact, the creation of printed books effectively augmented the materials presented in the lecture environment. Good instructors cannot be replaced by technology, but they can become better by using technology effectively.

In 1898, when Thomas Edison invented the film projector, he said that it eventually would replace the classroom instructor. That did not happen. Instead, the film projector was a way of expanding the walls of the classroom and bringing in other resources. Although this was an effective new resource, it was clear that students still needed a classroom instructor to structure and guide learning and provide and manage interactions.

Early debates on instructional television followed the same course. Promoters of television thought the technology would eliminate the need to have classroom instructors. However, it soon became apparent that there was still a need to have an instructor available to interact with students and structure and facilitate the learning experience. The advent of the Internet will not lead to the replacement of instructors any more than did other technologies, but instructors will need to take on new roles. These new roles and the skills needed to fill them are discussed in detail in Chap. 7.

THE IMPACT OF INTERNET-BASED INSTRUCTION

The impact of technology is pervasive in almost every aspect of life. Look at the way people travel, work, and entertain themselves. For the past 20 years that impact has been less dramatic in the area of education and training, but the advent of the Internet has changed how people will communicate and train in the twenty-first century. The Web has changed many aspects of education and training. This firmly established technology is going to continue to create new and more powerful learning environments.

There are already many success stories regarding Internet-based learning programs. Not only are these programs cost-effective, they are educationally effective as well. Internet-based technologies allow people to deliver information anytime, anywhere, and in a form convenient for the students. Students like this channel of interaction because it is less threatening to many of them than is face-to-face interaction and gives them an opportunity to reflect more on their answers.

Another impact of Internet-based instruction is the emergence of global universities and national universities that can deliver programs to people anywhere, anytime, and in a form convenient for the student. Students will no longer have to think about participating in a single college program in their own geographic locations. Instead, they can select the best programs and the best faculty members and take courses that meet their needs. In fact, in the twenty-first century it may be more common for students to take many courses from many different universities than to take all their courses at one university. In this way students can customize an educational program to meet their specific needs and interact with the best minds in the world to learn a new educational discipline or shape their understanding of current challenges.

This situation will be especially prevalent in advanced and professional education. Students with unique needs stemming from their business environment may not be able to find the expertise they need locally. With Web-based distance learning technologies, they have access to world-class subject matter experts who can help them fulfill their educational objectives and personal development requirements. The Web has changed everything!

INTERNET EXAMPLES AND CASE STUDIES

AT&T and Lucent Technologies have successfully used technology-based training delivery systems for years to offer programs to geographically dispersed employees. We now describe two of the challenges these organizations faced and the distance learning solutions they developed to meet them.

Business Challenge.   Alan Chute remembers the pressures that led to the just-in-time model of training that his company adopted. The company developed a just-in-time model because of critical business drivers and individual students' needs. Whereas in the past it could rely on more traditional, same-time, same-place training delivery systems, the need for training and retraining is much more acute than it has ever been before, and traditional approaches have become inadequate for meeting this need. One reason is that with the global competition companies are challenged with increased time-to-market pressures. Organizations have to shorten cycle times and need to get information to people on a much more timely basis. Organizations are also looking for ways to be more cost-effective in their delivery. The traditional channels of bringing everyone together were very time-consuming and costly. Companies not only sustained massive travel costs but also suffered a loss of productive time while people were en route.

Both AT&T and Lucent have gone beyond the same-time, same-place model to a more varied approach that includes a broad range of options to choose from, depending on the learning situation. Much of their synchronous same-time, same-place distance learning is conducted via audioconferencing and videoconferencing. They also have the option of providing synchronous distance learning through the Internet with streaming audio technology. Another option is the different-time, different-place training system, what is called a just-in-time knowledge system. With this approach the student and the instructor never come together at the same place or at the same time, yet they freely exchange information with each other by using a variety of asynchronous technologies. The instructor "hosts" the information or course content that the students need; the students in turn access it, study it, formulate their questions, and then, through asynchronous interaction, communicate with instructors and other students. Below we describe two examples of innovative distance learning solutions that AT&T and Lucent Technologies implemented to meet their educational and training needs.

Solution I: Call Center Institute. Lucent Technologies' Call Center Institute (CCI) offers its worldwide call center sales and service employees Internet-based knowledge resources and knowledge-sharing opportunities to help them learn. CCI specialists are responsible for consulting with Lucent customers as those customers cost-justify, design, develop, and implement their own call center and transaction center solutions.

Call centers are business operations that combine voice communications and data-processing technology that enable an organization to implement critical business strategies or tactics aimed at reducing costs or increasing revenues. Physically, a call center is a place where a group of people handle large volumes of incoming or outgoing calls for the purpose of sales, marketing, customer service, telemarketing, technical support, and other specialized business activities. For example, banks, insurance companies, and investment firms use call centers to enable customers to transfer funds, initiate investments, order and activate automatic teller machine accounts and credit cards, check account balances, verify credit, confirm transactions, and so on. A call center typically is set up as a large room with workstations that include a computer, a voice terminal connected to an automatic call distributor, and one or more supervisor stations. The call center may stand alone or be linked with other call centers. It also may be linked to a business data network that includes mainframes, microcomputers, and LANs. In summary, call centers are powerful and complex operations; as a result, Lucent's call center specialists need sophisticated skills and up-to-date knowledge to effectively design and implement solutions for their customers.

Staying current on the technology that supports call centers is a formidable task; it is even more challenging to survey and understand the wide range of innovative call center solutions available today. Within Lucent Technologies, the CCI internal Web site is regarded as the source of knowledge and knowledge sharing for call center intelligence. CCI created comprehensive Web sites with over a thousand documents and graphics and 500 Mbytes of information on current call center technologies and applications. The site hosts case studies, white papers, research articles, training materials, PowerPoint presentations, demonstration software, performance support tools, and so forth. Through a common Web browser, call center specialists can access these knowledge resources any time and anywhere. They also can share knowledge with other associates worldwide through the community of practice idea-sharing utility. In addition, call center specialists can participate in synchronous interactive teleconferencing programs, Web-based seminars, and telecollaboration consultations that enable them to interact directly with Bell Labs experts.

Synchronous interactive learning experiences permit a student to sign on to a program hosted on the Web. These programs follow a "60-minutes" format with segments dedicated to key topics of interest to call center specialists. Each segment has a 10-minute executive overview that includes the statement "For more information go to CCI URLs"; each segment also includes 5 minutes of planned questions and answers. The program overview and content are hosted at the CCI Web site before, during, and after the "CCI Live" teleconference. The entire program can be hosted, delivered via streaming audio, and then stored for future replay on the CCI web server.

The regularly scheduled live (synchronous) sessions focus attention and pull people through the self-paced CD-ROM and taped
(asynchronous) components of the CCI curriculum. These synchronous teleconferences and other planned synchronous learning experiences—face-to-face seminars, audio and video teleconferences,
and the like—account for approximately 20 percent of the time people spend in CCI learning activities. The other 80 percent is spent
in asynchronous learning activities, including participation in Web-
based courses, reading white papers and case studies, preparing pro-
posals, and completing on-line Web-based testing activities.

In addition to the knowledge warehouse and training programs
created for Lucent's call center specialists, CCI has created knowledge resources for a network of worldwide Lucent distributors and
for external customers as well. The distributors gain right of entry to
the CCI extranet site by accessing the site's URL and then entering
a unique ID and password. There they can obtain nonproprietary
information that enables them to better perform in their role as
Lucent distributors.

External customers also can access the URL (http://www.lucent.
com/CCI) to obtain a wealth of call center–related information provided by Bell Labs, national centers, professional organizations, and
various sources within Lucent Technologies. These information and
knowledge resources have been useful to customers in researching
and planning call center solutions. Customers also have an opportunity to identify additional resources that are valuable to them so
that the CCI Webmaster can include appropriate links in the CCI
resource listings.

Solution II: Center for Excellence in Distance Learning.
Another organization that has used the Web successfully to disseminate its knowledge resources is the Center for Excellence in Distance
Learning (CEDL). CEDL resources have been developed by AT&T
and Lucent Technologies teleconferencing specialists in response to
their internal needs and to customer-identified information needs
related to increasing productivity, reducing costs, and enhancing
quality in their educational and training organizations. The result is
an extensive information and knowledge resource for anyone who is
planning distance learning programs.

Hundreds of documents that provide information on the design
and implementation of distance learning solutions are hosted at this
award-winning site (http://www.lucent.com/cedl). Additionally, the

most frequently asked customer questions are addressed. Following are several commonly asked questions:

1. Why is distance learning becoming so important?
2. Which organizations have implemented distance learning?
3. Which technologies are available?
4. What implementation steps are recommended?
5. Which organizations provide support for distance learning?
6. What funding programs are available?

The materials available at this Web site include published articles, white papers, case studies, product information, and PowerPoint presentations. The site also provides a password-protected area called LearningWorks for Lucent Technologies customers. With an ID and a password, customers can gain access to detailed research abstracts and an on-line booklet entitled *Distance Learning: An Introduction,* which has hot links to a variety of distance learning resources.

The overall mission of CEDL is to advance the state of the art in distance learning. CEDL has collaborated with Bell Laboratories and leading universities to create an integrated approach to developing distance learning applications. The CEDL organization works closely with universities that are recognized leaders in the field of distance learning, including the University of Wisconsin–Extension (http://www.uwex.edu/disted/home.html), Penn State (http://www.cde.psu.edu/), and Indiana University (http://www.indiana.edu/~scs/homepg.html). The partnership between CEDL and these universities has advanced both knowledge about and practice in the field of distance learning through the study and creation of innovative telecommunication solutions to today's education and training challenges.

ASYNCHRONOUS COMPUTER TECHNOLOGIES: ADVANTAGES AND LIMITATIONS FOR TRAINING AND EDUCATION

Most of the computer-based training options discussed above are based on asynchronous, or time-delayed, approaches to training. Many people see asynchronous forms of distance learning such as

Web-based training and instructional computer conferencing as exciting new ways to connect teachers, training content, and learners in relationships that will no longer be limited by time or distance. Not surprisingly, the reality of the situation is more complex. Although these forms of distance education and training offer major benefits as channels for learning, like any other instructional medium, they have limitations as well. Understanding both the strengths and the limitations of asynchronous forms of distance learning can help you make informed decisions about their appropriateness for meeting *your* needs.

Although one site of asynchronous communication, the WWW, is a relative newcomer to the training arena, the concept of computer-based asynchronous learning is not new. Both computer-based training and instructional computer conferencing have been used for a number of years as primary or supplementary delivery channels. As a result, educational researchers have been able to study the characteristics and effectiveness of these forms of asynchronous instruction and form some general conclusions about their potential advantages and limitations.

ADVANTAGES

Communication that is asynchronous is time-independent. In other words, learners using asynchronous training media are not limited by anyone else's schedule or convenience; they have 24-hour-a-day access to data, information, and people. This feature is particularly attractive to working adults, most of whom have to juggle multiple roles: worker, parent, spouse, for example.

Asynchronous training, like other forms of distance education, is also place-independent, meaning that learners are not limited to resources—human as well as informational—that are physically near them. Information stored on the other side of the globe is as readily accessible as is information in the next office, and colleagues around the world are as available for collaboration as are those across town. This characteristic of asynchronous distance learning makes it particularly useful in incorporating cross-cultural perspectives and resources into distance education and training.

Asynchronous distance learning is also more self-paced than is traditional face-to-face instruction or training. Because there is no pressure to answer or respond immediately to the instructor or to other learners, participants can take the time to think more deeply and completely about their responses. This feature of asynchronous communication can make these forms of learning particularly responsive to individual differences among learners. For example, learners with a more thoughtful, reflective style of thinking and responding need not be overshadowed by their more quick-thinking or quick-talking "eager beaver" peers. The additional time for reflection that asynchronous communication fosters can also result in interchanges that are more thoughtful and well considered than those seen in traditional classes.

Finally, the technological characteristics of asynchronous computer-based training offer a number of benefits in terms of affordability, course management, and skills that are particularly relevant in an increasingly technological society. First, the combination of telecommunications and computer technologies is relatively inexpensive because it uses equipment and services (computers and telephone service) that are widely available in most workplaces. Second, the combination of hardware, software, and telecommunications services needed for instructional computer conferencing supports a variety of course management functions: organization and distribution of materials; formation and oversight of small work groups, discussion areas, and bulletin boards; archiving of discussions; assignment submission and return; and management of student records. Third, the technological nature of these forms of distance training reflect the changing environment of today's workplace. Increasingly, workers at all levels need to be able to use and interact comfortably with an array of computer and telecommunications technologies. Receiving workplace training via these technologies encourages and reinforces the development of skills that are necessary or useful in a variety of workplace situations.

POTENTIAL LIMITATIONS

Not surprisingly, many of the advantages discussed above represent trade-offs that must be carefully balanced in making decisions about the media used for training. For example, the time-independent feature of asynchronous learning is certainly beneficial to busy adults juggling multiple roles. However, it can be a drawback in situations in which information processing or problem solving has to progress quickly. In the same way, the self-pacing benefit of asynchronous learning can become a disadvantage when learners are unwilling or unable to be self-motivating or self-directing or when organizational policies or schedules limit the amount of time available for an educational or training experience.

The technology itself can impose limitations on its usefulness or appropriateness for some training purposes. For example, technically unreliable systems and poorly designed, "user-unfriendly" software can hamper the actual delivery of training and prevent the development of a positive attitude toward training among the participants. A related problem arises when the participants—both instructors and students—have not been adequately oriented to this new method of education or training delivery. Unless the participants feel comfortable with this method of teaching and learning, its use will be a distraction that shifts the focus from the content that is to be learned.

Particularly in today's business environment, one cannot always rely on traditional face-to-face ways of teaching employees because of cost pressures and scheduling conflicts. More and more organizations are relying on just-in-time knowledge systems where course information is delivered electronically at a time and place convenient for the student; E-mail and other, more elaborate forms of computer-based interactions, such as those discussed above, are changing both the way people do their work and the connections they form with others in the process.

However, as the discussion in this section suggests, a distance learning solution involves more than just picking a technology and using it as a new way to conduct business as usual. Maximizing the benefits offered by these new ways of delivering education and training depends on understanding the concept of a distance learning *system* and attention to the factors that contribute to the success of an organization's distance learning solution. Chapters 4 through 8 discuss these topics in detail.

FURTHER READING

The following two sources provide in-depth information about the categories of computer conferencing summarized in this chapter.

Berge, Zane. 1997. Group computer conferencing: Summary of characteristics and implications for future research. In E. Wagner and M. Koble (eds.) *Distance Education Symposium 3: Course Design*. University Park, PA: American Center for the Study of Distance Education, The Pennsylvania State University.

Santoro, G. 1995. What is computer-mediated communication? In Z. Berge and M. Collings (eds.) *Computer mediated communication and the online classroom.* Volume 1: *Overview and perspectives*. Cresskill, NJ: Hampton Press.

THE DISTANCE LEARNING SYSTEM

MORE THAN A COLLECTION OF HARDWARE

Realizing the exciting potential of distance learning depends on more than just combining innovative technologies to deliver content. Only through careful planning and implementation based on the idea of the distance learning context as a system in itself rather than an add-on to an existing system can an organization maximize the benefits of distance learning.

A SYSTEMS PERSPECTIVE ON DISTANCE LEARNING

Distance learning systems often are perceived on two levels. In more superficial perception a distance learning system is seen as an integrated combination of technologies—print, voice, computer, and/or video—used to transmit or deliver instruction or training to learners and provide opportunities for interaction between the instructor and the learners and among the learners. However, this view treats one part—the technology—as if it were the whole system. From this perspective, all that is needed to update a training program is to add the latest "gee-whiz" technology while otherwise following more or less the same training or educational procedures that were used before. Unfortunately, when an organization looks at distance learning systems in this way, its decisions can become equipment-driven rather than needs- or results-driven and the outcomes are likely to be disappointing.

Realizing the potential of distance learning requires a broader, more comprehensive view of distance learning systems. The system is not a technological framework into which learners, content, instructors, and other elements are placed unchanged. On the contrary, each of these elements is an integral, interrelated part of the system and brings needs as well as contributions to the overall shape and potential of the system.

ELEMENTS OR COMPONENTS OF A DISTANCE LEARNING SYSTEM

Although many distance educators agree on the need to view a distance learning system from this expanded perspective, they often give different names to these elements or components or suggest a somewhat different emphasis within the system as a whole. Some system models focus on elements of process; however, the generic list of system components presented here focuses on the people and things that are important elements of the system: learners, content, "process people" (designers, instructors, managers, support staff), communications technologies, and organizational context. When these elements are combined in mutually beneficial and supportive ways, providing for the facilitation and support of the interactions between and among these components, a successful distance learning system is developed. Let's look at these elements individually and see how each one interacts with other parts of the system.

LEARNERS

It may seem too obvious to say that learners are part of a distance learning system. However, it is not just the learners' presence but also the characteristics and needs they bring with them that influence the design, structure, and operation of a distance learning system. These characteristics and needs influence the system as a whole in at least two ways. First, system processes must be designed to meet learners' needs and take into account their learning characteristics. Second, learners' thoughts and actions within the system will exert an influence, since any action in one part of the system cannot help influencing (in at least a small way) the other parts.

The extent to which learners exert influence on a distance learning system depends somewhat on the characteristics of the system, such as its size, setting, and purpose. For example, a smaller learning system is more likely to be influenced by the needs of individual learners than is a very large system. Similarly, a system, such as a secondary school, intended specifically to serve learners' general educational needs is more likely to be influenced—or at least be influenced in different ways—than is a system designed to train learners to perform a task or function to meet organizational goals.

CONTENT

Content, or subject matter, is another obvious element of a distance learning system. Content is a main focus or object of both the learner's and the instructor's activity, and on a superficial level distance learning systems may seem to exist for no reason other than to bring learners and content together. However, as with learners, content is a more complex element of the system than one might at first think. Content, like learners, has characteristics and "needs" that influence the development and operation of a distance learning system. For example, effective teaching of some types of subject matter may need to incorporate high-resolution visual images to adequately represent or display the concepts or skills being taught. In this case, the distance learning system has to include a technology that can reliably transmit such images. Other educational or training content may require little or no visual reinforcements but be highly dependent on real-time audio interactions such as those supported by audioconferencing.

This intersection of the needs of the content with the capabilities of the technologies must be an important consideration in designing distance learning systems. If decisions about delivery technologies are made without careful consideration of the "needs" of content, the quality of the educational or training activity is likely to suffer, with negative effects on both the learners and the credibility of distance learning as an educational or training alternative.

ORGANIZATIONAL CONTEXT OR SETTING

The organizational context of a distance learning program has a strong influence on its ultimate shape or identity. First, this context will determine the purpose or purposes for which people are being brought together to learn a particular content or range of content (e.g., information, knowledge, skills). In purely educational environments, for example, students' learning needs as developing individuals and members of society determine the focus of any educational program, including programs delivered at a distance. These settings both allow and encourage the fairly broad range of approaches and outcomes that result from differences in students' characteristics, needs, and interests. In other organizational contexts, such as business and industry, the focus of distance learning is of necessity somewhat different. In these contexts training, including distance training, is highly responsive to the needs and characteristics of the organization rather than those of the individual learner. Although some accommodation can be made for individual differences, the main focus of training is to teach the task-oriented skills and knowledge necessary for the effective operation of the organization.

Second, the organizational context exerts an influence through its commitment of tangible and intangible resources to a distance education or training program. The extent of philosophical or "moral" support offered by the leadership of an organization has a tremendous impact on both the character and the ultimate success of a program. Leadership decisions relating to the placement of a distance learning program within the overall structure of the organization will influence the attitudes of all those in the organization who are affected by the program. More pragmatically, the level of leadership support, as reflected in the commitment of financial resources, will determine the types as well as the extent of distance learning programs that can or will be implemented.

PROCESS PEOPLE

This component includes professionals who design, implement, manage, and support the various aspects of a distance learning system. These professionals can be roughly divided into two groups: those directly involved in the learning interaction, such as instructors, and those involved in the support of the system as a whole or the support of specific components of the system. The second group includes instructional designers, counselors and other student support staff, administrators and administrative staff, and technical design and support staff. In small organizations with relatively small distance learning systems, one or two people may fill all these roles. However, larger systems in large organizations that must take advantage of economies of scale usually have a higher degree of role specialization.

The makeup of this component will change as the distance learning system matures and changes in response to a constantly changing environment. For example, the type of person needed to guide the development and implementation of a new distance training program within an organization may not be the same type of person needed to lead the program through a relatively quiet period of stability and consolidation. Additionally, the relationship between the process people and the other elements in the system—as well as the dynamics within this component of the system—will change over time as new organizational needs arise and the other components of the system change.

COMMUNICATIONS TECHNOLOGIES

Obviously, delivery technologies are important elements in a distance learning system. These are the mechanisms that allow one to extend instruction beyond the confines of the classroom, loosen the constraints traditionally imposed by time and place, and place distant resources within the reach of learners and instructors. Important as these technologies are, however, we have listed them as the last element of a distance learning system to emphasize the point that technology should not be the determining factor in decisions about the development of a distance learning system.

Each technology or combination of technologies has strengths and weaknesses that make it more or less appropriate for a particular learner population, content area, or organizational setting. Ideally, the choice of technology—or even the decision to use no technology—should be based on a consideration of the characteristics and needs of the learners, the content, the organizational context, and the process people in the educational or training system. However, because we are talking about a real-world, interrelated, interdependent system, we understand that this prescription cannot always be filled. Often, the elements of the system are less than perfectly balanced and one element exerts a disproportionate influence on the decisions made within the system. Thus, budget limitations may prohibit the purchase of the most appropriate delivery technology for a particular educational or training need, or an organizational leader may make a unilateral technology decision to which all the other components of the system must adjust as best they can. Still, to the extent possible, an organization should try to avoid a technology-driven focus on its distance learning system.

For the purpose of clarification, we have presented each component in a distance learning system as an isolated element. However, when these four elements are appropriately balanced, they support and strengthen each other. In other words, it is in the *relationship* and *integration* of these elements that the true identity and power of a distance learning system become apparent.

FURTHER READING

The view that distance learning solutions are systems is being more widely discussed in writings about distance learning. The following two sources by recognized experts in the field of distance education informed our thinking and discussion on this topic:

Duning, B. S., M. J. Van Kekerix, and L. M. Zaborowski. 1993. *Reaching learners through telecommunications.* San Francisco: Jossey-Bass.

Moore, M. G., and G. Kearsley. 1996. *Distance education. A systems view.* Belmont, CA: Wadsworth.

GETTING STARTED IN DISTANCE LEARNING

Is Your Organization Ready?

Hundreds of business case studies have demonstrated that distance learning can effectively address the needs of geographically dispersed employees who have continuous learning requirements. Distance learning solutions work

- When an organization wants to keep professionals up to date on new technology, capabilities, regulations, and certification requirements

- When an organization wants to provide basic skills and knowledge training to new or entry-level employees

- When an organization wants to train its sales force or other remote people in new products, policies, tools, and procedures

- When an organization wants to train its customers in new products, provide support, and increase satisfaction

- When an organization wants to provide its employees, wherever they are located, with equal access to career training and development as well as opportunities to enhance their basic skills and become more productive

Regardless of the reason why an organization is considering distance learning, it is necessary to take some very simple steps up front to ensure success during the implementation of the learning solution.

One of the most important steps in the development of a distance learning solution is the process of obtaining a clear understanding of the range of organizational and user needs that will be met by the system. A high-quality needs assessment provides the data required for identifying key locations and educational needs to be served, solution planning, cost-benefit information, system design, system use, and system expansion. Equally important, a needs analysis helps ensure that once the company's system has been installed, it will be used because it meets the requirements and reflects the culture of the organization. Finally, the needs assessment provides data for the eventual expansion of the system.

In addition to assessing needs, it is important to assess the readiness of the organization to accept the changes that will result from adopting a distance learning system. Important components of organizational readiness include current levels of technology infrastructure, administrative procedures that can be adapted to support distance learning, and the compatibility of the organization's business strategy with the implementation of a distance learning solution to education and training needs.

A distance learning needs and readiness analysis may take different forms, depending on an organization's size, the geographic distribution of its employees, existing travel and communication patterns, and management style. Similarly, the responsibility for the preparation of such an analysis may vary considerably from organization to organization. A good way to start is to look within the organization for existing models that were used to implement other multisite systems in the past. This will help you frame questions for interviews and focus on the data an organization typically requires for business case preparation. The sources of data are generally organizational reports, user surveys, and interviews with those who will be affected by the distance learning system.

ASSESSING ORGANIZATIONAL NEEDS AND READINESS

You should start the needs assessment process by reviewing internal organizational reports that discuss current issues and challenges and identifying gaps in employees' skills, evaluating training effectiveness, and monitoring training travel costs. You also should review case study reports of other organizations that have identified training problems and addressed them with distance learning solutions, such as those maintained at the Web site of the Center for Excellence in Distance Learning (http://www.lucent.com/cedl/). These reports can help you generate questions to use in the interviews and surveys you will conduct with managers, support staff, and future users of the organization's distance learning system.

PERFORMANCE NEEDS ANALYSIS: IDENTIFYING CONTENT FOR THE CURRICULUM

You cannot determine the content of a distance learning program until you have the results of a performance needs analysis. This analysis can identify performance problems and/or needs and their root causes. Individual performance problems generally occur because individuals do not have the knowledge they need to perform a task, do not know how to perform a task, and/or do not have the tools they need to perform a task. A very simple method for categorizing performance problems is to ask three questions:

1. Is the performance problem related to lack of knowledge?
2. Is the performance problem related to a skill deficiency?
3. Is the performance problem related to lack of the appropriate tools?

Once you have determined the type of performance problem, you need to examine the appropriateness of distance learning for meeting the identified need. Ask yourself, Does a training solution to this problem already exist? What might a distance learning approach add to the solution of the problem? Other important questions are, Does distance learning reduce the costs associated with delivering the learning? Does it improve the speed of delivering the learning? Does it increase the quality of learning by standardizing the delivery?

Some of your answers will depend on whether your organization uses a centralized classroom delivery approach or a decentralized field delivery—train-the-trainer—approach. If it uses a train-the-trainer approach, you probably will develop very detailed instructor manuals and materials and rely on field employees to deliver the training. One advantage of distance learning is that it allows the information on which learning is based to be disseminated quickly. A second advantage of distance learning over a train-the-trainer approach lies in the reduction of costs: Fewer people deliver the training, and fewer instructor materials must be produced. Also, distance learning allows an organization to use a few well-trained expert instructors to deliver most of the training. The train-the-trainer approach, by comparison, depends on the varying abilities of field employees to deliver instruction, and regardless of how well training information is documented, difficulties with quality often result from the individual characteristics of an instructor's skills and the instructor's ability to deliver the training as specified by the manual.

PERFORMING A TECHNOLOGY ASSESSMENT

Before you begin to determine which technologies are appropriate for your particular performance needs, you need to ask, What technologies do we currently have in place that would support a distance learning initiative, and how can I get access to them? The scope of the distance learning initiative and the influence of the executive stakeholders will determine whether you install a completely new distance learning system or use the existing technological infrastructure.

The current status of the organization's technology infrastructure has a significant impact on the choice of technology for the distance learning initiative. Although the most important factor in the choice of technology should be learning requirements, technology decisions often are made on the basis of availability. Deploying new technology for an initial distance learning initiative is risky and often costs more than an organization is willing to spend. In situations in which distance learning is new to the organization, building on the existing technology infrastructure is often the wisest course of action. In this way, both the expenses and the "tension" resulting from the changes brought about by distance learning will be minimized.

Table 5-1 can assist you in doing a technology assessment. Answering yes to any of the questions in the table indicates that the organization has experience with that distance learning technology and probably can support a distance learning initiative with that technological platform.

Another approach to making technology decisions is shown in Table 5-2. This tool can help you select a distance learning technology that meets the organization's needs.

ADMINISTRATIVE ASSESSMENT

Administrative considerations regarding distance learning center on the key areas of distribution of materials, registration and tracking

TABLE 5-1. Sample Technology Assessment

QUESTION	YES	NO
Does the organization currently conduct multisite meetings by speakerphone?		
Does the organization currently have an embedded base of personal computers accessible by the target audience?		
Does the organization use CD-ROM technology?		
Does the organization use electronic mail or electronic bulletin boards?		
Does the organization conduct one-way video meetings?		
Does the organization conduct multisite interactive video meetings?		
Does the organization use Internet or intranet technology?		

of participants, and management of technology and facilities. In assessing the organization's readiness to implement a distance learning program, consider the following questions:

1. Do you currently distribute learning materials to the field? Can you use the same procedures for distance learning?

2. Do you have a registration system for your current training delivery? Can you use the registration system for a distance learning program?

3. Do you certify employees on the basis of training completed? Will you certify participants who complete distance learning programs?

4. Are the locations to which you would like to deliver the program designed and equipped for distance learning? (See Chap. 8 for information that will help you answer this question.)

5. Do you currently schedule conference rooms, both locally and in remote locations, through a central function? Do you need to modify the scheduling procedure for distance learning (see Chap. 8)?

6. Do you have an administrative staff to support the current training? Will it be able to handle the additional workload needed to support the distance learning programs?

7. Do you have individuals who can be contacted in remote locations for assistance in the administration of a distance learning program?

TABLE 5-2. Technology Decision-Making Tool

IF	AND	THEN
The organization currently conducts multi-site meetings by speakerphone	Your learning objectives require live interactions between participants and do not require non-verbal cues	Consider a distance learning application which uses audio tele-conferencing supported by print materials
The organization currently uses personal computers and/or CD-ROM technology	Your learning is self-paced	Consider a distance learning application which uses computer-based training (CBT) or electronic performance support system (EPSS) technology
The organization uses electronic mail, bulletin boards, and/or Internet-type applications	Your learning requires interaction between participants	Consider a distance learning application which uses network-based CBT, EPSS, chat room, and/or bulletin board technology
The organization currently conducts one-way video broadcasting	Your learning requirements specify a need to see live demonstrations	Consider a distance learning application which uses one-way video broadcast technology
The organization currently conducts multi-site video meetings	Your learning requirements specify a need to interact visually	Consider a distance learning application which uses interactive video technology

These questions, while fairly simple, represent very important considerations in the effective implementation of a distance learning program.

IDENTIFYING THE COMPANY'S BUSINESS STRATEGY

No matter how good it looks on paper, a distance learning solution will not be effective if it does not fit into the strategic framework of the organization. Organizations have characteristic approaches to reaching their goals, and otherwise viable solutions may not be accepted if they do not reflect those strategic approaches. For this reason, as part of the assessment of organizational readiness you will want to identify the organization's business strategy.

Treacy and Wiersema[1] identified three different and distinct business strategies employed by market leaders. Table 5-3 is a tool that will assist you in identifying the organization's business strategy. Put a check next to the statement that best describes the company's business strategy. Respond to each question by writing the response number in the column to the right.

Operational Excellence (Score of 4–6).   If you responded yes to the first question in Table 5-3 and your total score is between 4 and 6, your organization's business strategy is probably one that focuses on operational excellence. Organizations that have operational excellence as their chief strategy deliver a combination of quality, price, and ease of purchase that no one else in the market can match. They execute exceptionally well, and their value proposition to their customers is a guaranteed low price. Because these companies focus primarily on lowering costs, they must have tightly controlled processes that avoid waste, a decision structure which is centralized, and measurement systems that assess compliance with norms. Operationally excellent companies rely on efficient transactions to improve productivity and ensure high-quality customer service. The development of people in these companies focuses on preparing them to execute the organization's policies and procedures in a consistent and predictable manner. Distance learning applications appropriate for this business model need to provide decision support, just-in-time information in terms of policy and procedures, and knowledge and skill development that supports compliance with business performance standards.

Product Leadership (Score of 7–9).   If you responded yes to the second question in Table 5-3 and your total score is between 7 and 9,

TABLE 5-3. Business Strategy Qualification Checklist

BUSINESS STRATEGY	RESPONSE NUMBER
Respond to the following questions by writing the number that corresponds to your choice in the column to the right.	

Which of the following processes does the organization emphasize?

1. Efficient product and/or service supply and basic service that minimizes costs and drives down the product and/or service price
2. Innovative product and/or service development and delivery and speed to market
3. Retention of customers by maintaining a relationship with customers' specific needs and focus on sustaining a strong relationship

Which of the following operating principles best describes the organization?

1. Standardized, simplified, tightly controlled operations which are centrally controlled and centrally planned
2. Loosely knit business structure that is highly volatile and entrepreneurial, focusing on highly innovative products and services
3. Employees who are self-directed and empowered to make decisions to meet the specific needs of their customers

Which of the following management systems does the organization focus on?

1. Integrated, reliable, high-speed transactions with a strong emphasis on compliance with specified standards
2. Results-driven management systems that measure and reward new product and/or service success and tolerate trial-and-error development
3. A system that focuses on creating results for carefully selected and nurtured customers

Which of the following best describes the organizational culture?

1. A culture that continuously seeks to eliminate waste and reward efficiency
2. A culture that encourages individual creativity and a desire to create the future
3. A culture that embraces specific versus general solutions and is sustained by strong and lasting customer relationships

Total

your organization's business strategy probably emphasizes product leadership. Organizations that have product leadership as their chief strategy deliver innovative products to the marketplace. They must rely on the creativity of their people and the speed at which they can move their products to market. Product and service life cycles are extremely short. The development of people in product leadership companies needs to focus on providing them with challenging projects that stimulate their creativity and continuously motivate them to "beat the odds" by producing products or services that others claim cannot be delivered. People in product leadership organizations have a strong drive to solve problems and a stronger drive to beat bureaucracies. Distance learning applications appropriate for this business model need to facilitate creative idea generation, the dissemination of new ideas, and competitive intelligence in order to develop innovative products and services.

Customer Intimacy (Score of 10–12).   If you responded yes to the third question in Table 5-3 and your total score is between 10 and 12, your organization's business strategy is probably one that focuses on customer intimacy. Organizations that have customer intimacy as their chief strategy deliver products and services to meet specific customer needs. These organizations emphasize building customer loyalty and trust rather than having the most innovative product or the best price. The challenge these organizations face in developing their people is to recruit, assimilate, and retain talented people who can understand the changes customers are facing and provide them with products and services specific to their needs. Distance learning applications appropriate for this business model need to provide employees with specific information on and specialized product and/or service support for individual customers (see Table 5-4).

THE USER NEEDS ASSESSMENT

We believe that one of the most important steps in the development of a distance learning solution is the process of obtaining a clear understanding of the range of needs and requirements of individual users of the system. Earlier in this chapter we discussed the importance of assessing the organization's readiness for distance learning. Here we focus on the importance of understanding the requirements and motivations of the participants in the distance learning program.

TABLE 5-4. Business Strategy and Distance Learning Technology Matrix

	OPERATIONAL EXCELLENCE	PRODUCT LEADERSHIP	CUSTOMER INTIMACY
Individual learning • Print • CBT/CD-ROM • EPPS • Web-enabled hyperlinks	• Standardization of operating procedures • Decision support • Product information • Delivery of functional and technical knowledge	• Decision support • Product information • Delivery of functional and technical knowledge	• Decision support • Product information • Delivery of functional and technical knowledge
Group learning • Internet/ intranet chat rooms and bulletin boards • Audio and audiographic teleconferencing • Video teleconferencing	• Development and support of customer service best practices • Development and support of operations best practices	• Determining innovative product and service requirements • Creative problem solving • Sharing of ideas	• Determining customer-specific product and service requirements • Creative problem solving • Sharing of ideas

User requirements define the technological capabilities a distance learning system must provide. Whether you are establishing a small distance learning system with as few as two sites or a multinational system with hundreds of locations scattered across multiple time zones, you will need a good understanding of user needs and requirements.

IDENTIFYING THE SYSTEM'S USERS

You first need to identify the people who will be directly affected by the distance learning system. People who will be involved with the system in one way or another include the business leaders, the human resources managers, the training managers, instructors, the MIS/Telcom managers, the support staff, and the employees who will be the students served by the system.

Decisions regarding who will use and be affected by the distance learning system will be made by many people; however, especially in the early stages of planning and development, you may want to target particular groups that will make successful implementation more likely. For example, the first projects of your distance learning system should be designed to serve users in key roles and in departments where the system is most likely to deliver high-visibility benefits, in other words, areas where it will have the best chance of success. Look for individual managers or operational units that are feeling some pain because they cannot meet current training demands because of constraints on time and human resources. Choose training requirements that have not been satisfied well or are not being addressed at all in the current system. You want the success of the distance learning program to be evident to the entire organization. Ensure that the upper management of each unit is an integral part of the process; management's continuing participation and support will be vital to the ongoing development and success of the program.

UNDERSTANDING USER REQUIREMENTS

All those affected by the distance learning system will have a point of view regarding the issues and challenges they face. It is better to identify and make plans to address these concerns up front than to wait until they have been revealed in a project debriefing report.

Avoid the temptation to "cut to the chase" by asking directly, Which distance learning technology do you think will best meet your needs? This approach does not reflect the preferred interview process of enumerating the organizational, unit, or employee requirements first and then systematically developing a recommendation. Any good project manager will state that efforts during the first few days (or weeks if you are designing a very large distance learning system) should be focused on uncovering user requirements. Try to understand expressed and unexpressed user requirements before beginning to suggest or prescribe technological solutions.

Here is a set of questions we have used to uncover what key individuals think distance learning will do for them and the company. The answers to these questions can provide valuable insights into the concerns, motivations, and needs of a system's potential users.

- *What are the existing or emerging issues and challenges facing you and the company today?* When thinking about these issues, consider the following factors:

  Goals and strategy

  Competition

  Markets and customers

  Technology

  Regulations and policy mandates

- *What implications do these issues and challenges have for the organization?* In other words, how will the company and organization deal with these issues and challenges? What strategy will be chosen, and which actions will be taken? What must the company or organization do, do better, or do differently to compete and succeed?

- *What implications do these issues and challenges have for you and your unit?* Are your employees adequately prepared for these issues? If not, what are the knowledge areas, skills, or other characteristics that will be necessary for success in the future?

- *What will a high-performing employee of the future do differently?* What specific characteristics will high performers have that set them apart from average performers? How will these characteristics continue to evolve?

- *How will employees of the future acquire and maintain the knowledge and skills they need to succeed?* What will the organization do to keep its employees motivated, informed, and fulfilled in their jobs? What technologies will the employees use to access the information they need to do their jobs and learn new skills?

- *What additional information do you believe is important?* Please share any other information that you believe is relevant to your preparation for distance learning.

These questions can serve as a starting point to determine the underlying challenges the individual employee, the unit, and the organization will face, and the answers can help focus the implementation activities you will plan for the distance learning system.

Throughout the needs assessment process, try to get detailed information about specific educational requirements that exist in the targeted units. When you design and implement the company's distance learning system, you will in effect be offering users a solution to problems they have in performing specific tasks and achieving specific results. Therefore, it is important to know beforehand what those tasks are and what those results are intended to be. As you collect information from many individuals, you probably will find considerable overlap. This information will allow you to begin to design distance learning applications that work well horizontally, across the enterprise.

A high-quality needs assessment is the first step in developing a solid basis for the design, use, and expansion of a distance learning system that will meet current and future individual needs and organizational challenges. The next step—managing the change process within the organization—requires equally careful attention to ensure that the system you develop is accepted and used effectively by the organization as a whole.

MANAGING ORGANIZATIONAL CHANGE: BUILDING ACCEPTANCE FOR THE DISTANCE LEARNING SYSTEM

Business is living through some of the most unsettled times in history. This turbulence in the work environment is caused by significant changes in organizational strategy, people, methods, and technology that are occurring so fast that the workforce often is unable to adjust and operate effectively. When you consider introducing any change, especially one as significant as distance learning, you also need to consider the impact of that change on the parts of the organization that are directly or indirectly affected by it. Essentially, distance learning affects three critical areas in an organization: people (training staff and learners), the learning process, and technology. The extent to which you carefully manage these areas throughout the change process will determine how successful the distance learning experience will be.

People in an organization generally behave in ways that are accepted by the organization; that is, their beliefs, behaviors, and assumptions are consistent with the organization's norms. Most trainers still believe that instructor-led training in a classroom is the only effective way to deliver training, and many training organizations continue to measure their effectiveness by the number of bodies in seats and the length of the waiting list to attend training. They believe that a good course is one that has a large number of attendees and a large waiting list, and their reward system is based on these measures. Similarly, most learners state that they prefer classroom training: It is what they are used to and comfortable with.

To effectively introduce distance learning into an organization, you need to understand what people's attitudes and behaviors are now, what you would like them to be, and the process needed to encourage and support the desired changes. Process and technology changes are relatively easy compared with the changes *people* must undergo to implement distance learning successfully. People are by far the single most important factor in bringing about any kind of change, including the adoption of a distance learning system.

THE CHANGE PROCESS

In 1958 Kurt Lewin[2] developed a simple model to describe the change process, and that model is still considered one of the most accurate representations of how change occurs. The model depicts change as a series of transitions between the current state (status quo) and the future state (desired change). The transition state represents the phase of change during which people begin to adapt to the change. A frequently used metaphor for this process is the transformation of ice to water and back to ice. The ice must be melted into a liquid, and the liquid must be frozen (reshaped) into ice. In organizational change, the "melting" is the transition period between the current state and the desired state; it is the time during which the people involved in the change realize the impetus for change (see Fig. 5-1, which has been adapted from Ref. 2).

According to Daryl Conner,[3] the motivation for people to move from the current state to the future state is the realization that the cost of the current state exceeds the cost of the transition. Because change is disruptive, expensive, and time-consuming, it cannot be approached casually. A change such as the implementation of a distance learning system will be successful only if the people affected by it realize that its potential value is greater than that of maintaining the status quo.

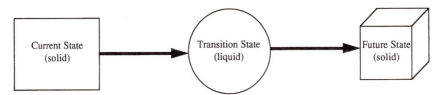

FIGURE 5-1.   The change process.

In other words, the question, What's in it for me? will be in the minds of people at all levels of the organization. Although this question often remains unspoken, it needs to be taken seriously and answered thoughtfully since it represents all the concerns and anxieties that people faced by change feel but may be unable or unwilling to express. By anticipating this question you will be better prepared to address concerns, manage expectations, and oversee the process of change that will accompany the institution of a distance learning system in your organization.

ROLES IN THE CHANGE PROCESS

The people in an organization fill three important roles in the change process: change stakeholder, change agent, and change target.[3] The change stakeholder is the individual or group with the organizational power to legitimize the change, the change agent is the individual or group responsible for implementing the change, and the change target is the individual or group whose knowledge, skills, attitudes, or behaviors will be altered as a result of the change.

These three roles always exist formally or informally in any change project and each contributes to its success or failure, yet many people still lack an understanding and appreciation of the importance of these roles in the overall change process. It is especially important that those charged with implementing a new iniative understand the relationships between the roles and work to coordinate the efforts of key people. Without thoughtful direction, the interactions between the roles can become imbalanced or fragmented: Stakeholders attempt to initiate major organizational change by issuing a "decree" to the change targets, bypassing the change agent's implementation role; change agents decide to modify a plan without ever gaining the stakeholders' approval or attempt a change far greater than what the stakeholders intended; or, as is more often the case, change is initiated without a clear definition of the target population, how those in it will be affected, and to what extent they are likely to accept or resist the change.

Understanding and managing the nature and interdependence of the three roles is a key element in successfully managing change. Table 5-5 gives an overview of the characteristics and importance of each of these three roles, which are discussed in greater detail below.

Stakeholders.   As Table 5-5 illustrates, the stakeholder's role is important in each phase of the change process. The stakeholder is

TABLE 5-5. Change Management Roles

| | PROCESS STEPS | | |
ROLES	CREATING MOTIVATION FOR CHANGE	TRANSITION	STABILIZING AND/OR INTEGRATING CHANGE
Stakeholder	Most important	Most important	Most important
Change agent	—	Most important	—
Change target	—	—	Most important

the one who sets the stage for change and sustains the change. Unfortunately, stakeholders sometimes initiate a change and then seem to disappear, a behavior that sends a confusing message to the change targets and may lead them to question the organization's commitment. Because of the frequent—almost daily—changes in organizations today, stakeholders should be involved in every phase of the change process. To sustain the effort, stakeholders also must be able to identify and solicit active support from different functional areas and different levels in the organization—to make others into stakeholders. This approach, which is often referred to as cascading stakeholdership, recognizes that since change must be implemented at the employee level, "buying in" at that level is as important to success as is identifying the executive stakeholders. One primary reason change efforts fail is a lack of "ownership" at the middle management and employee levels. Our experience with implementing new distance learning programs supports the idea that those at different levels of the organization should be viewed as having a stake in the project.

How can the primary distance learning stakeholders be identified? Because distance learning has an impact on the organization's people, processes, and technology, distance learning initiatives often require coordination of implementation activities that cross organizational functions. The primary stakeholder or stakeholders should be people who have direct authority over the functions you need to work with to implement the distance learning initiative or are in a position to build the relationships needed to obtain cross-functional support. Stakeholders have to believe in the change and be strong advocates; they also need an in-depth understanding of what the change means and its long-range implications. Before undertaking any distance learning initiative you must identify the stakeholders and understand their level of commitment to the project.

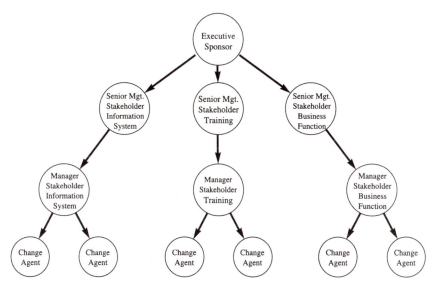

FIGURE 5-2. Stakeholder relationships.

It is often useful and sometimes critical to map out stakeholder requirements before initiating a distance learning initiative. Figure 5-2 shows a stakeholder "map."

Change Agent. Most change efforts fail not because the change lacks value for the organization but because the change agent failed to communicate the benefits of the initiative across the organization's functional boundaries and build the necessary support at different levels of the organization. The change effort most frequently breaks down at the user or change target level. The change agent must have a clear understanding of the benefits the user will derive from the distance initiative and be able to communicate those benefits effectively.

Change Target. Two primary user groups or change targets are affected by a distance learning initiative: the training organization and the learners. Each group will resist the change, and the form that resistance takes will be characteristic of each group. Similarly, the benefits that result will be specific to each group. You will need to ensure that both the concerns of and the benefits for each group are addressed.

The training organization's primary basis for resistance typically centers on the belief that distance learning is not as effective as traditional classroom instruction. Often this concern is related to a fear of having to learn to develop and deliver training via new technology. Benefits to the training organization include reaching more learners, having more frequent opportunities to deliver training, and reducing travel costs.

Resistance by individual learners often is based on their familiarity and comfort level with classroom learning. These individuals also will resist distance learning if they are not given time during working hours to complete the training. Typical benefits to this group from participating in distance learning include less costly training, more time spent on the job, shortening of the learning curve, faster dissemination of information, improved job performance, and the potential for special recognition and rewards. Learners who are aware of the potential benefits of distance learning are much more likely to accept the new approach willingly. The time investment you make up front to discuss the reservations participants may have and clearly communicate the benefits of the new system will pay off handsomely in the long run.

MATCHING TECHNOLOGIES WITH LEARNING REQUIREMENTS

How people learn (internalize the knowledge or skill) and why people learn (motivation) are the same in both distance learning and classroom learning. In both cases, how the learning experience is structured is an important factor in whether that experience is a positive one. For people to accept the change represented by distance learning, their educational experiences need to be both effective and satisfying.

An important element in structuring satisfying learning experiences is matching the specific attributes of the technology with the learning requirements of the content, the learning objectives, and the characteristics of the learner population, as specified in the curriculum plan. Similarly, you need to decide which format—individualized instruction or group learning—is appropriate for a given situation or content. Table 5-6 can provide guidance in this selection process.

Some learning requirements may be best met by using an integrated approach. For example, introductory or prerequisite learning activities could be delivered via the technologies appropriate for individual learning before the learners participate in group learning activities that focus on more advanced content.

Another technology consideration relates to the storage of the content for a distance learning program, including general information resources. Large volumes of content such as policy and procedure manuals, as well as content dependent on video, are best stored on diskettes or CD-ROM. Content that is stable or does not change frequently also can be stored on diskettes or CD-ROM. If the content is volatile or requires learner real-time interaction with

TABLE 5-6. **Distance Learning Technology Selection Tool**

	INDIVIDUAL LEARNING ENVIRONMENT	*GROUP LEARNING ENVIRONMENT*
Knowledge	• Print • CBT (diskette or CD) • Performance support tools • Web hyperlinks	• Audioconferencing • Videoconferencing • Web chat rooms
Skills	• Print • CBT (diskette or CD) • Performance support tools • Web hyperlinks	• Audio teleconferencing • Video teleconferencing • Web chat rooms
Tools	• Performance support tools • Web hyperlinks	• Web bulletin boards

other learners, a networked distance learning approach should be considered. Table 5-7 provides some general guidelines related to the issue of local versus networked content.

Carefully matching learning requirements with delivery technologies will promote successful learning experiences which in turn will facilitate the change process. When identified needs are addressed in appropriate and effective ways, the innovation represented by the new distance learning system will be much more readily accepted and used within the organization.

PROJECT MANAGEMENT

Two common reasons for project failure are insufficient planning and poor project management during the change and implementation phases. Because of the complexity of distance learning initiatives, in-depth project planning and project management are imperatives. Distance learning initiatives typically require the coordination of at least three different organizational functions: business functions, information systems functions, and training functions.

For example, when a major insurance carrier initiated the development and implementation of a distance learning program, four primary stakeholders were involved: the office of claims, whose personnel were the targets; the information systems organization, which owned the technical platform; the state organization within which the distance learning initiative was to be piloted; and the training department. Careful planning and coordination across functions were required to ensure the project's success.

TABLE 5-7. **Distance Learning Technology Platform Matrix**

	LOCAL	NETWORKED
Individual learning environment	Use diskettes or CD-ROM if the content	Use a LAN or the Internet/ intranet if the content
	• Is stable and does not change frequently • Uses multimedia • Is large in terms of volume	• Is volatile and changes frequently • Requires maintenance of its security • Requires tracking learner compliance
Group learning environment	Use diskettes or CD-ROM	When the content requires real-time interaction between participants, use networked distance learning technologies such as
	• If the content is a prerequisite to a group learning experience • To reduce the amount of time spent in the group learning experience • To allow more time for group interaction during the group learning experience	• Audiographic teleconferencing • Video teleconferencing • Internet/intranet chat rooms

Developing a Project Charter and Work Plan.   One of the first steps in project planning is understanding who the executive stakeholder is and the project's scope. We have seen far too many projects that lacked adequate stakeholder support. When a project team is unable to answer the question, Who cares if this project is completed? the project is probably doomed. Another common problem is lack of clarity regarding a project's scope. You need a guide to determine when you have finished a project and have met the stakeholders' expectations. One way to mitigate these risks is to prepare a project charter.

After the project charter has been approved, the next step is to assemble the project team and develop a project work plan. The project plan details the specifics of how the project will be managed, identifying the project's stages, tasks, responsible persons, and dates for the completion of tasks and stages. Develop a work plan that meets your needs, including as much detail and specificity as is needed to complete the project successfully. A number of software tools are available to assist you in developing a work plan. Table 5-8 illustrates some of the basic components of these plans.

TABLE 5-8. **Distance Learning Work Plan**

STAGE	TASKS	DELIVERABLES
Assessment	• Determine how the distance learning initiative supports the organization's business strategy • Assess learner needs: knowledge, skills, tools, readiness for distance learning, motivation • Assess training staff's readiness (instructors and developers) • Determine management's requirements • Assess current state of technology infrastructure • Assess current curriculum's potential for conversion to distance learning • Determine measurements required • Determine administration's requirements • Determine administrative requirements	Distance learning assessment document that includes complete documentation of the results from the assessment stage and a recommendation to continue or stop the initiative
Design	• Design distance learning content: knowledge, skills, tools • Design instructor and developer workshop on distance learning • Design management's requirements • Design distance learning technical infrastructure • Design evaluation system required • Design administrative organization and performance requirements	Design documents for • Distance learning content • Instructor and developer workshops • Technical infrastructure • Measurement system • Administration organization

TABLE 5-8. (*Continued*)

STAGE	TASKS	DELIVERABLES
Development	• Develop instructor and developer workshop on distance learning • Develop distance learning content: knowledge, skills, tools • Develop management's requirements • Develop distance learning technical infrastructure • Develop measurement system required • Develop administrative organization and performance requirements	• Instructor and developer workshop on distance learning • Distance learning materials • Change management strategy and plan • Software developed and equipment identified • Measurement system • Administrative organization and performance requirements
Implementation	• Develop instructors' and developers' distance learning skills • Distribute distance learning content: knowledge, skills, tools • Implement management's requirements • Deploy distance learning technical infrastructure • Implement measurement system required • Staff and train administrative organization	• Instructor and developer received orientation • Content delivered • Change management process implemented • Software, hardware, and network operational • Administrative staff recruited and trained

All the elements discussed in this chapter enter into the decision to choose a distance learning solution. Table 5-9 combines the most important questions relating to performance, technology, administration, organizational business strategy, user needs, and the change process into a tool that can provide an overview of the organization's readiness to adopt distance learning.

TABLE 5-9. **Distance Learning Readiness Assessment**

QUESTIONS	YES	NO
Performance Needs/Content		
Have you identified the performance problem to be addressed?		
Can you segment your performance problem into one or more of the following categories?		
• Things people need to know		
• Things people need to do		
• Things people need to do their jobs (tools)		
Does courseware currently exist which supports the improvement of the performance problem?		
Have you determined the distance learning technology based on individual performance requirements?		
Technology		
Have you assessed the current technical infrastructure?		
Have you determined the feasibility of using the existing technical infrastructure for the distance learning system?		
Does the organization have a history of successfully implementing systems projects?		
Administration		
Have you determined the administrative requirements to support the distance learning system?		
Have you determined the administrative requirements needed in remote locations?		
Have you assessed the facilities in the remote locations that will be used for distance learning?		
Have you determined funding for improvements to remote facilities?		

TABLE **5-9.** (*Continued*)

QUESTIONS	YES	NO
Business Strategy		
Is the reason for considering distance learning linked to the organization's long-term or short-term strategy?		
Have the benefits of implementing a distance learning system been documented?		
Can you link the distance learning benefits to specific business performance measures?		
Learner Assessment		
Do you have a record of the learner's prior training or educational experiences?		
Do you know the comfort leavel of the learner's with technology?		
Change Management		
Do you have a stakeholder for the distance learning initiative who is able to gain cross-functional support?		
Have you determined the level of acceptance or resistance to the distance learning initiative in the training department?		
Have you identified people in the training department who are more willing than others to embrace the distance learning system?		
Have you identified the benefits of the distance learning system for the learners?		
Do you have a performance management system in place that will reinforce the implementation of the distance learning system?		

NOTES

1. Treacy, M., and Wiersema, F. 1995. *The discipline of market leaders: Choose your customers, narrow your focus, dominate your market,* New York: Addison-Wesley.
2. Lewin, K. 1958. Group decision and social change. In E. E. Macoby, T. N. Newcomb, and E. L. Hartley (eds.) *Readings in social psychology,* New York: Holt Rinehart, and Winston.
3. Conner, D. R. 1993. *Managing at the speed of change: How resilient managers succeed and prosper where others fail,* New York: Villard Books.

DESIGNING A DISTANCE LEARNING SYSTEM

There are three main considerations in designing the structure of a distance learning system: equipment, communication services, and facilities. We discuss each consideration separately, with general material presented first, and then move on to design considerations that pertain specifically to distance learning systems based on specific technologies.

SYSTEM EQUIPMENT

Audio, audiographic, video, and Internet-based distance learning all require different equipment. What is selected for a distance learning system will depend on the end users' requirements. We have provided functional descriptions of the types of equipment needed for audio teleconferencing, audiographic teleconferencing, video teleconferencing, and Internet-based distance learning. However, we have refrained from recommending specific vendors' products because product features change and new products are introduced annually. Instead, we have provided a listing of the major vendors of audio, audiographic, video, and Internet distance learning products in Appendix B. We have also provided uniform resource locator (URL) links (World Wide Web "addresses") where you can obtain the most current product information available.

AUDIO SYSTEMS

Audio (voice) teleconferencing equipment includes terminals, telephone sets, microphones, and loudspeakers. Each of these four basic components plays a particular role in the system. In selecting a specific item in each component category, you will find a variety of products to choose from, and your decision will be determined largely by your ability to match specific product capabilities with your organization's needs. Following is a brief description of the four audio component categories, along with some operational considerations for product selection.

Terminals.   The terminal equipment is the heart of an audio system and provides the power and circuitry that enable the system to function. This equipment provides the capability to support microphones and loudspeakers. The number of microphones, coupled with the amplification capability of the loudspeakers, should determine the maximum size of the teleconferencing room and the number of participants that can be accommodated effectively.

Telephone Sets.   The telephone set allows students to initiate calls to other locations and receive calls originating from other locations. In some systems it also may provide certain control functions, such as incoming volume control and microphone muting.

Microphones.   Each training room should be equipped with one or more microphones to pick up the voices of all the students in the room. Voice pickup range varies from 18 in to 12 ft, depending on the system. The number of microphones required depends on several factors, including microphone sensitivity, room size, and the number of students to be served. The choice of microphones available for teleconferencing purposes is extensive, and these products vary widely in sensitivity, directional patterns, and other characteristics.

Loudspeakers.   One or more loudspeakers in each teleconferencing room are necessary for all students to clearly hear the amplified voices of other students at remote locations. The number of loudspeakers installed depends on power output, room size, physical placement, and the number of participants. Loudspeakers should be placed to allow maximum separation between loudspeakers and microphones to minimize the feedback that results when microphones pick up incoming sound. Several appropriate products are available, with the principal differences among them being power output and the type of installation, that is, ceiling-mounted, wall-mounted, or tabletop.

Criteria for Selection.   The criteria for selecting audio system components include quality of transmission and reception, flexibility of the system, convenience of controls, and a variety of special features. Audio systems can vary considerably in their overall capabilities and characteristics. Wide variations are possible in price and quality, portability, and the size of the conference room or user group that can be accommodated, although additional microphones and speakers usually can be added to the initial system at a later time if they are needed.

As you select the audio components for your system, keep the following considerations in mind:

- The system must be capable of allowing students to speak without raising their voices and to listen without straining.
- The system should provide transmission levels and reception quality that will allow speech to sound as natural as possible.
- For effective interaction, the system should be capable of providing fast "voice switching," the feature that controls the exchange of conversation so that only one location is transmitting at a time.
- The system should be able to accommodate a later increase in the number of microphones and/or loudspeakers.
- Microphones should have a muting feature so that side conversations can be held without disrupting the instructional session.
- The system should have an incoming volume control to allow the participants to adjust the incoming audio signal to a comfortable listening level.
- There should be an indicator light or another visual signal to inform the students that the microphones are active.
- All user control functions should be readily accessible and easy to use.

Careful selection of audio equipment, together with proper acoustic treatment of the training room, will result in a system with optimal audio performance. This system will afford the highest-quality audio obtainable over any type of network—including the public telephone network and private lines—through a standard telephone connection. It also will ensure maximum convenience, effectiveness, and comfort for the system's users.

Case studies can provide useful information for determining a company's need for distance learning equipment. The following example shows how one company deployed audio equipment in its distance learning facilities. Of course, the choice of equipment components and room design configurations *you* select will depend on your unique user requirements.

AUDIO DISTANCE LEARNING EXAMPLE

The marketing organization of a large company established an audio distance learning system that delivers weekly one-hour marketing update programs to keep the sales force up to date on products, services, and competitive offers.

The initial programs in 1982 were delivered to dedicated audioconference rooms at five regional headquarters sites. The dedicated conference rooms were equipped with built-in audio-conferencing systems with multiple microphones attached to conference tables, ceiling speakers, and sound amplifiers. The average cost for the audio teleconferencing system and installation was $10,000. Graphic support for the audio programs consisted of printed materials that were mailed to the remote locations.

In the second year of operation the distance learning system expanded to 35 branch office locations. Dedicated audioconference rooms were not always available, and so students used standard conference rooms equipped with high-quality portable speakerphones, each of which cost $2000. The speakerphones were placed in the center of the conference tables and connected to standard telephone lines. Graphic support for the programs was mailed or faxed to the remote locations.

Today over 400 locations participate in the network's audio update programs. The students use a variety of audio speakerphones that cost as little as $150 each, although there is a network stipulation that even these inexpensive speakerphones must have mute buttons so that local noise at the remote locations does not come across the network. Mail, fax, and/or E-mail are used to deliver graphic support for the programs. The price of audio teleconferencing equipment has dropped so dramatically that virtually any location can afford to become part of the company's audio distance learning system.

Audiographic Systems

The term *audiographic teleconferencing* refers to an "audio plus graphics" communications capability. Other terms related to this function include *document conferencing, whiteboard conferencing,* and *freeze-frame video teleconferencing.* Audiographic teleconferencing can provide the interactive exchange of printed documents, hand-drawn information, charts, slides, viewgraphs, still-frame video images, and so on. Although the audio portion of an audiographic teleconference is identical to an audio teleconference, a variety of additional equipment is needed to support the graphic capabilities. Following are several different types of audiographic interactions and the types of equipment necessary to support each one.

- *Interactive writing.* Interactive writing equipment, such as a whiteboard, enables instructors to illustrate the points made in their presentations, much as they would if they were writing on a dry marker board or flip chart in a face-to-face program. Diagrams and figures—including complex multicolored images—can be drawn at one site and received by the other sites, where they can be modified or erased by the participants at those sites.

- *Document conferencing.* Advances in personal computers and computer graphic capabilities have created a high level of sophistication in interactive document conferencing systems. This equipment enables students at several locations to collaborate on a shared document or graphic that is then automatically updated at all the sites involved.

- *Still video images.* Objects, documents, and other visual aids— even still images of people—can be captured by a camera and transmitted as part of audiographic teleconferencing. The images are recorded in the form of "electronic snapshots" on personal computers and then transmitted over normal telephone lines to other sites, where they are displayed on video monitors.

The following example describes an organization that adopted an audiographic distance learning solution; this example shows some of the equipment choices that are possible in using this medium for distance training.

AUDIOGRAPHIC DISTANCE LEARNING EXAMPLE

An engineering training division of a company established a 100-site audiographic distance learning system to deliver engineering and operations training courses throughout the organization. The remote locations were all equipped with a system for transmitting both audio and graphic information from one location to another over normal telephone lines. Each of the conference rooms had a lockable audiovisual cart that housed a speakerphone, personal computer, 26-in color computer monitor, writing tablet, and special modem that could send voice and data simultaneously on a single telephone line.

The rooms used for audiographic teleconferencing were set up like standard conference rooms with oval tables to facilitate interactions within the group and enable students to pass the writing tablet among group members. The equipment cart was positioned at one end of the oval conference table so that all the students could see the monitor easily. The cost of the audiographic distance learning equipment and the cart was $12,000.

VIDEO EQUIPMENT

A video teleconferencing system includes the equipment needed for the transmission and reception of motion video. It also may include auxiliary audiovisual equipment for enhanced presentation capabilities. We discuss both types in this section and offer some guidance in regard to equipment selection.

A wide range of products available from a number of different suppliers can meet your specific needs. General categories of video equipment include coder-decoder (CODEC) signal processors, room controllers, cameras, monitors, microphones, and loudspeakers.

CODEC.   A signal processor, otherwise called CODEC, is the single most important piece of equipment in a video teleconferencing room. Its function is to convert the analog signals generated by the room equipment into digital form and compress those signals for transmission on a digital service transmission channel. At the receiving end, the function of the CODEC is to reconvert the digital signal to analog form for reception and display by the room equipment.

Room Controller. A room controller is a device that enables the instructor or a student to operate the room's equipment from one spot. Most of these units are in the form of a keypad with a series of buttons designated for specific functions. The unit also may be in the form of a touch-sensitive video monitor containing symbols for the various functions.

Selection should be based on an evaluation of which one is most suitable for an individual company's intended applications. It is also important to locate the room controller in a place that is easily accessible; wireless keypads are very popular for this reason.

Video Components. The video equipment in a typical video teleconferencing room consists of a variety of specialized cameras and monitors. The number and types of these units depend on how large the room is, the number of students expected, and the kinds of activities that are most likely to take place.

Audio Components. The audio equipment in a typical video teleconferencing room consists of specialized microphones and loudspeakers. As with the video equipment, the number and types depend on the size of the room, the number of people who will participate in video teleconferences, and the expected activities.

Auxiliary Equipment. In addition to transmitting and receiving the pictures and voices of the teleconferencing students, many video teleconferencing rooms are equipped for the sharing of support materials. This equipment, much of which is identical to the equipment found in an audiographic teleconferencing room, can include the following:

- Facsimile machines for transmitting paper documents.
- Personal computers for the presentation of many of the graphics and charts used in video presentations. Most graphic images are created on personal computers (PCs), and so it makes good business sense to save the expense of creating intermediate media such as slides and transparencies when it is possible to electronically transmit the computer graphic image directly to the video teleconferencing system.
- A scan converter to allow the user to display graphics from a computer on a television monitor. The scan converter will convert a PC's Video Graphic Array (VGA) or Super VGA (SVGA) digital signals to a National Television Systems Committee (NTSC) ana-

log signal so that all remote participants can view the computer graphics on their television monitors.

- Videocassette recorders (VCRs) to make a permanent record of the proceedings. VCRs also are used to incorporate video segments into multisite teleconferences.

Questions to Consider in Selecting Video Equipment.   Certain questions about how the system will be used may have to be answered before you make the final equipment selection. The equipment marketed for use in a video training facility covers a broad spectrum of products, functions, designs, and technical specifications. Before you begin the process of selecting the equipment for your company's video teleconferencing room, answer the following questions, which focus on key issues of video equipment selection.

Do you want to be able to connect your video teleconferences and training programs to other companies' facilities and with publicly available facilities?   If you intend to hold video teleconferences between the video teleconferencing rooms on your company's premises and the rooms of other companies or rooms that are publicly available, it is necessary to determine the video standards for each CODEC used. This consideration is critical because the picture processors marketed today can vary in terms of signal compression methods and are not all compatible with each other. A good tactic is to insist that all the video systems be ITU H.320 video CODEC standards-compliant. This will ensure the interchangeability of different manufacturers' CODECs.

How important is it that the equipment in the video teleconferencing rooms be "transparent" to the system's users?   Normally, every effort should be made to make the equipment in video teleconferencing rooms as user-friendly and unobtrusive as possible, because the participants typically have little experience with or interest in technical matters. When even technically trained employees are in the role of learners, they can be distracted by equipment that is imposing in appearance or complex in operation. You can achieve maximum transparency by keeping much of the room's equipment out of the view of students (see the discussion of room design, below). Another way to make the system transparent is to select a room controller that can be used easily by the instructor and the students. Make sure that the table and/or remote control units you choose are appropriate for the way the system is intended to function.

What types, sizes, and shapes of video monitors should the system have, and where should they be placed?   A variety of video monitors are available for video teleconferencing use. Your selection will depend on several factors, including the size of the group, the types of graphics that will be used, whether you need simultaneous display of people and graphics, whether you need high-resolution graphics, economic considerations, and the personal preferences of the principal user groups. Following are some of the most common monitor configurations.

- *Incoming monitor.*   The incoming monitor is used primarily for the display of incoming images of teleconferencing participants but also can be used to display graphic images. In addition, this monitor can display images of people and graphics simultaneously by using techniques such as a split screen or an insert of a person's "picture" over a portion of an image of graphic material in much the same way that captions for the hearing-impaired are inserted into the corner of a television picture. This monitor also can display the incoming and outgoing images at the same time by using a picture-in-picture (PIP) technique. If the system is going to provide only a continuous visual overview shot of a group of the students at the distant location, the monitor should be big enough that viewers can see facial expressions clearly. A large-screen video projector is especially valuable in displaying such group pictures. The principal incoming monitor generally is placed on the front wall, directly facing the students, and positioned to provide the maximum sensation of direct eye contact with the students at the distant location.

- *Outgoing picture monitor.*   The outgoing monitor allows the instructor to see the images that are being transmitted to other sites. When camera switching is taking place, outgoing monitors allow the instructor to know exactly which image is being transmitted to other sites. Also, these monitors allow students to see others in the same room without having to turn their heads to look at them directly. In many installations, portable or roll-about video teleconferencing systems are used. In this case, a single monitor is used for the incoming video signal and the outgoing picture is placed in a PIP window. In other rooms, two monitors are used and the incoming and outgoing monitors are identical in size. The location of outgoing monitors varies considerably from company to company.

- *Preview video monitors.* Additional video monitors may be used in association with special equipment to preview graphic materials or images. These monitors allow the instructor to call up and position the material that is about to be transmitted.

What should the incoming monitor display? The incoming monitor should display one of the following:

- An overview of the entire group at the remote location ("continuous presence")
- A close-up or medium shot of the person at the transmitting location who is speaking or, if no one there is currently speaking, the one who last spoke
- Either of the above at the option of the instructor

Each alternative has specific advantages. An overview picture allows the instructor to see all the students at the distant location simultaneously and observe everyone's reactions to the discussion no matter who is talking, a feature that is important to many instructors. Also, some people find that switching to close-up pictures each time a new speaker begins to talk can be distracting and even disorienting. Finally, a system that provides only a single overview camera at each location is considerably less expensive than more elaborate systems.

However, a close-up picture allows the instructor and students to interpret the expressions of the person who is speaking to a much greater extent than does an overview shot, enhancing the speaker's ability to communicate, especially in situations involving persuasion. The system in which close-up pictures are used must include a means of switching from one close-up to another as the speaker changes. In some systems the close-up camera covers two or three of the students, offering a compromise between the benefits afforded by overview shots and true close-up shots and keeping distracting camera switching to a minimum.

If close-ups are used, should the required camera switching be automatic or manual? Manual switching from one close-up camera to another normally requires the constant attention of a technician, which is both expensive and distracting to the participants. For this reason, switching usually is accomplished automatically through the use of a voice-switching system. The close-up camera covering the person talking is automatically activated by the room controller when a voice signal is received from that person's microphone.

Switching between overview and close-up modes can be done manually, at the option of the instructor, or automatically. For example, the camera may be activated automatically if no one in the room has spoken for a given period. Many systems have both manual and automatic switching systems, and the instructor selects the mode to be used.

When auxiliary cameras are used, the instructor or presenter generally employs manual switching so that there is no risk of interrupting the presentation of graphics material through the activation of cameras when students make side comments or when there is other noise in the room.

What sort of graphic material will be transmitted, and in what manner? If your company's video teleconferencing needs are like those of most other companies, you will want to have the option of transmitting and receiving images of graphic material. Such material can include hand-drawn diagrams, artwork, easel cards, flip charts, viewgraphs, slides, and three-dimensional objects such as package designs, product samples, and models. The type of graphic material you intend to transmit will affect the choice of equipment. Following are descriptions of various types of graphic materials you may need to transmit and equipment considerations related to each type.

- *Small flat artwork, diagrams, and typed or printed materials.* The transmission of documents, images, charts, graphics, small three-dimensional objects, and similar materials can be accomplished with a portable document camera. By focusing a document camera on the material and transmitting the image, you can make sure that all sites can see the materials. Zoom controls are provided for close-ups of materials. This camera can be freestanding, or it can be part of a special graphics display. In the second case the graphics display unit can be mounted in the conference table or located elsewhere in the room, away from the table.
- *Large artwork, maps, easel cards, flip charts, and handwriting and/or drawing.* Transmitting images of large materials normally requires an auxiliary camera. Such units may be tripod-mounted portable cameras or wall-mounted cameras. The instructor can

control camera zoom, panning, and tilting. In addition, a multi-functional monitor often is used with such units to allow a presenter to see and adjust—off line—a picture that is about to be transmitted. The head in some document cameras can pivot so that the unit can be used as an auxiliary camera in the room.

- *Viewgraphs and other transparent materials, including slides.* Color or black-and-white viewgraphs and slides can be transmitted by means of a document camera equipped with a light box to illuminate a transparency from below.

- *Videotapes.* Some companies provide videocassette recorders in their teleconferencing rooms to allow all the locations involved in a teleconference to view copies of the same videotape simultaneously. While technically not a transmission from one location to another, this practice allows the sharing and discussion of videotaped material.

What types of microphones should you select? Your objectives in selecting microphones should be to provide the highest-quality sound possible from the system and give the users the least obtrusive equipment that will meet your video teleconferencing needs. Feedback loops and ambient room noise are of particular concern in this connection. The microphones should be capable of preventing the incoming audio signals from being retransmitted. The microphones also should be able to suppress ambient noise such as paper shuffling and air-conditioner rumbling. Some microphones are designed to screen out ambient noise by having a highly directional pickup pattern; these microphones can be placed on the conference table or built into it and aimed directly at the user's mouth. Other microphones suppress unwanted sound by having a "close talking" pickup pattern. They are worn close to the user's mouth by means of a clip, chain, or crook. Microphones should have the capability of being turned on and off manually, allowing students to carry on private discussions without interrupting the program.

How many loudspeakers should there be, and where should they be positioned? You should install enough loudspeakers to ensure that all students and observers are able to hear clearly. Their placement will depend on the size and shape of the room, but they should facilitate the participants' ease of listening regardless of their location.

Will you ever need to keep a permanent record of a video teleconference?   If you anticipate keeping a permanent record of a video teleconference, a videotape recorder can provide a full-color, full-motion copy of the entire program. Copies of graphics or documents that were presented in the program can supplement the videotape.

Should the system be designed to ensure the privacy of video teleconferences?   The use of public switched network services for a video distance learning program ensures that the program will have the same level of security as a normal telephone call. You can achieve added security through the use of encryption equipment located on the premises. Such equipment is available from several manufacturers, normally as an optional feature of a CODEC.

How many students will normally participate in the program?   The type of video terminal equipment needed depends on your typical program. For programs with three or more students participating at each location, a group video system is appropriate; for programs with only one or two people at each site, desktop video systems may be appropriate.

Desktop PC video teleconferencing systems use high-end 486 and Pentium computers with a camera and a microphone mounted on the monitor to allow for video and audio interaction between people. PC video teleconferencing also permits shared software interaction. The users may collaboratively use a whiteboard utility and share software applications such as word processing, spreadsheets, and presentation software. Some systems may have high-resolution video-graphic computer monitors or projectors. These monitors allow the display of a wide range of computer graphics as well as the display of standard video signals, such as the NTSC output of a VCR or camera.

Can a graphics tablet be used for drawing?   Many PC-based graphics systems use a graphics tablet instead of a mouse and keyboard as the main control device for presenting computer graphics functions. Graphics tablets allow instructors to advance the pages of a graphics slide show, point to items on the screen, and use the drawing area as a whiteboard for interactive on-line writing.

The following video distance learning example provides an example of appropriate equipment choices for meeting a common organizational training need.

Video Distance Learning Example

A sales training organization installed a two-way video distance learning system to conduct training in sales skills at 22 remote sites. The course topics included consultative skills, negotiation skills, and presentation skills. The system also was used for executive briefings and sales management meetings.

A roll-about video teleconferencing unit was used with a single 26-in monitor to display incoming and outgoing pictures. The sites all had cameras with pan, tilt, and zoom controls that could be operated locally or from the instructor's location. In this way the instructor could demonstrate a skill and then directly observe the behavior of the students during the subsequent role-playing exercise. The cost of the roll-about video teleconferencing equipment was $45,000. The price of alternative systems would range from $10,000 for a simple portable system that plugged into a television monitor and an ISDN line to about $70,000 for a large unit with a special instructor control panel for multimedia presentations.

Internet Equipment

The basic equipment required for participating in an Internet-based distance learning program is a PC. The computer can run on either the Windows operating system or the Macintosh operating system. For the purposes of this discussion, the computer will be referred to as a PC.

The PC can be a workstation, a desktop computer, a laptop, or a notebook computer. Students' PCs also need to have a sound card and speakers or headsets. The PC should be equipped with Web browser software that supports JAVA scripts, for example, Netscape version 3.0 or later and Microsoft Internet Explorer version 3.0 or later.

You also need to provide a means of accessing the company's intranet (internal network). Intranet access is generally available at all company work locations through the corporate local area network (LAN) or wide area network (WAN) or on a dial-up basis with a modem. To support the streaming audio segments included in some courses, the PC should be at least a 486; if a modem is used, it should have at least 28,800 bps speed. To support high-quality streaming video, the PC should be at least a Pentium and have a connection on the LAN.

The following example provides a typical intranet distance learning equipment solution.

INTRANET DISTANCE LEARNING EXAMPLE

A manufacturing company offers a range of professional development courses through its corporate intranet. The courses include topics such as diversity training, certified project manager training, and training programs on emerging technologies. Students typically register for the course on-line by providing a corporate identification number and then begin the course immediately. Testing also is accomplished on-line, and credit for completion is posted automatically to a student's employment record.

Each student has a PC or notebook computer, a Web browser, a sound card, and a means for accessing the company's intranet. The typical Pentium multimedia workstation the company deploys throughout the workforce costs $2500; the typical multimedia notebook costs $5000. Intranet access is generally available at all company work locations through the corporate LAN, or it can be accessed on a dial-up basis with a modem.

The course content, the streaming audio and video segments, and the testing programs are hosted on training department servers that are connected to the company's intranet. Each server has the capability of supporting 50 simultaneous users. E-mail communications among instructors and students are supported by the company's E-mail system.

COMMUNICATION SERVICES

Communications services provide the linkages in a distance education system by joining instructors to learners, learners to each other, and all the participants to a wide variety of resources. Most important, communications services provide the means for the interactions on which high-quality distance learning is based.

AUDIO AND AUDIOGRAPHIC BRIDGING

Devices called *bridges* are needed to tie together three or more locations participating in a teleconference. Bridging can be accomplished in several ways. The method chosen depends on the type of teleconferencing the company plans to use, the frequency of use, the locations to be connected, and other factors in the design of the company's system.

Multipoint communications services can be obtained from a service provider external to the company. You can also purchase bridging equipment that will be dedicated to the needs of your distance learning program. You also may be able to do small multipoint conferences by using bridging features designed into your company's private branch exchange (PBX) telecommunications system. Whichever approach you select, your telephone connection should be equal in quality and performance to that of a normal two-point telephone call.

Bridging Service Providers. Service providers offer an easy-to-use, high-quality method of connecting multiple locations. You can contact an operator to set up a teleconference call for you, or you can connect to other locations yourself for audio-only or audiographic teleconferences. You will need to contact a bridging service that is available through the public switched (dial-up) network or through the company's telecommunications department.

Dedicated Bridging. Many organizations purchase their own bridging devices once they determine that there will be enough use to justify a dedicated resource. As a general rule, if an organization begins to average several hundred port hours of teleconferencing a month, it is time to consider purchasing a bridge and hiring the organization's own operator.

PBX Bridging. Organizations that require more than just a few telephone lines usually employ a PBX. In simple terms, a PBX is an automated switchboard on which the organization's telephone operators assist callers only when required. Large organizations that use PBXs generally order them with teleconferencing bridges already built in. For example, one large PBX allows users to set up conference calls involving up to six locations by pushing "conference" on their desk telephones and then dialing up the numbers.

The most sophisticated audio and audiographic bridges enable users to select from a menu of call setup options. The "meet-me" capability permits all sites to dial into the bridge at a predetermined time; when they enter a security code at the prompt, they are automatically tied together in the teleconference. A "blast-up" capability allows the bridge to dial out to over a hundred users simultaneously. In addition to these automated capabilities, many bridges allow an operator or a person at the teleconference to control access during the program by adding or dropping individuals.

We recommend that organizations just starting out with distance learning contract for bridging services with an external or internal bridging service provider. In this way they can focus on the program design and delivery and rely on experts to handle the technical coordination of the program. After your initial pilot programs you may want to do the bridging yourself with a PBX bridging system, or you may decide to invest in a dedicated bridge to meet the teleconferencing needs of your distance learning program.

VIDEO COMMUNICATIONS SERVICES

Today a wide range of video communications service options exists to provide the telecommunications circuits for a distance learning system. High-capacity digital and compressed digital services are available to support a number of distance learning applications. The type of digital service you select for your system will depend on a number of factors, including types of use, frequency of use, quality requirements, and the location of the company's video teleconferencing rooms. Distance learning applications that use video technology fall into two general categories: one-way video and two-way video.

The distinguishing characteristic of a one-way video distance learning application is that video signals are transmitted only from the instructor to the learners. The most common method of transmission or broadcast is by satellite. The components of a satellite broadcast systems include the origination site, the satellite uplink for transmission of the program to a satellite orbiting the earth, the satellite transponder that receives the earth signal and retransmits it back to the earth, the satellite downlink equipment, and a site for people to view the program on standard television monitors.

A program that originates from one site is transmitted by satellite to a "footprint" that covers a very wide area. For example, satellite programs at one site in North America can be received simultaneously at a limitless number of sites anywhere in the United States, thus serving a geographically dispersed audience. Real-time interactivity among the sites and the originating location is accomplished by using telephones, student response keypads, and faxes.

A two-way video distance learning system provides video and audio communications in both directions between learners and instructors. All the locations in a two-way video system are equipped with cameras, monitors, and microphones. Point-to-point and multipoint connections enable instructors and learners to see and hear each other.

Compressed Video.   Compressed video systems offer the flexibility of a variety of bandwidth services to the user. The audio and video signals go through digital signal processing that reduces the amount of information that is sent from location to location. These compressed signals can be sent to virtually any location via satellite or over the switched telephone network. When switched digital services are used, the quality of the picture is a function of how much bandwidth is used. The bandwidth can range from 56 kbit/s to a full T-1 circuit of 1.5 Mbit/s. Satellite transmission paths are commonly 3.3 Mbit/s or 6.6 Mbit/s but can be as wide as 45 Mbit/s, a full transponder for analog video. The cost of the connection is based on the bandwidth used.

The most commonly used and most cost-effective transmission rate for distance learning systems is the Integrated Services Digital Network (ISDN) 128 Kbit/s service. Many organizations use this service because it is generally available in all metropolitan areas and because the access rate for the service is about the same as that for two normal analog telephone lines. The long-distance rates on ISDN calls are less than $30 an hour for a coast-to-coast call. Some distance learning organizations are using three ISDN circuits bonded together to provide a level of service of 384 Kbit/s. This rate can handle 30 video frames per second and deliver near-VHS quality in a video distance learning program.

Full-Motion Systems.   A full-motion video distance learning system is one that provides picture quality that is comparable to that of commercial television. These systems typically require an investment in fiber-optic cables, high-capacity circuits, or satellite transponder access to network learning sites together. Today full-motion network systems often are built with private, full-time, or part-time transmission paths to support them. In the future public broadband video networks such as Asynchronous Transfer Mode (ATM) will provide integrated multimedia communications at speeds exceeding 155 Mbit/s.

Multipoint Video.   Multipoint video, as the name implies, refers to programs that connect three or more locations. In the case of satellite video broadcasts, an unlimited number of locations can tune in to the distance learning program. The program offers only one-way video, and so the special considerations relating to multipoint video interaction are not an issue.

Terrestrial dial-up multipoint video programs accomplish bridging through the use of a multipoint conferencing unit (MCU). An MCU functions similarly to the audio bridge described earlier in this chapter. Most MCUs offer a number of video switching modes, including voice-activated (the person who is speaking is automatically seen at all locations), manual-controlled (the instructor selects which site is seen at all the other sites), and broadcast mode (the instructor is seen at all sites throughout the program even when remote students are asking questions).

As with audio and audiographic bridging equipment, MCUs can be installed on the premises with a PBX included or accessed from a network service provider. The selection of a multipoint video system is influenced by learning requirements and cost factors.

INTERNET COMMUNICATIONS SERVICES

International standards exist for the Internet Protocol (IP). Consequently, many developers have written software for and manufacturers have created hardware systems for IP. For this reason, the communications services for Internet-based distance learning are in many respects more straightforward to implement than are those for video distance learning systems.

You can access Internet-based distance learning resources through your company's internal Internet, its intranet. The company's MIS department will provide guidelines for accessing the company intranet, which is generally available at the company work locations through the corporate LAN or accessible with a modem for home office or traveling employees.

If your training organization hosts its content on the external Internet, you can access it through an Internet Service Provider (ISP). Hundreds of local and major national ISPs provide access to the Internet. The local telephone directory can help you find local ISPs, or you can contact national service providers such as America on Line and AT&T WorldNet to set up Internet accounts. The national ISPs generally have local telephone access numbers in all the major metropolitan areas. If an organization's employees travel frequently, having local access numbers across the country can save long-distance charges.

Most ISPs offer access at speeds of at least 28,800 bps. If you have a 33,600-bps or 56,000-bps modem, you may want to seek out an ISP that can accommodate the highest speed your modem permits. An important point, however, is that having a high-speed modem and an ISP that accommodates high-speed modems does not necessarily guarantee that the telephone line between you and the ISP will consistently deliver performance at the highest speed possible. Other line impairment factors, such as the quality of the wire, the distance between relays, and weather conditions can reduce the speed or the communication system.

FACILITIES DESIGN

Distance learning facilities should be designed to encourage maximum use. Equipment selection is only one part of designing a company's teleconferencing system. Today most group video systems are designed to be at least semiportable. The equipment may be semipermanently installed, or it may be placed on a large roll-about cart. If you select the roll-about cart option, make sure that the cart has a large television monitor securely mounted on top of it. A 26-in monitor is the minimum size; a 30-in or larger monitor is preferable.

You also may plan to design a dedicated video distance learning room for the company to use for training programs and/or business meetings. We recommend that you keep in mind that the effectiveness of the company's teleconferences will be diminished and usage may be curtailed if the equipment is not installed in a convenient and inviting location, if the size or shape of the furniture makes the room difficult to use, or if noise or improper lighting interferes with transmission or reception.

There are several options in setting up a distance learning training or teleconferencing room. You can use roll-about video teleconferencing equipment that can be moved from room to room, modify an existing space, or build a new room designed expressly for teleconferencing. You can serve as your own contractor, making the decisions about room design and equipment selection yourself, or select an equipment supplier that provides a total package of services and products, including room design and construction. Whichever approach you choose, you will need to take the following design considerations into account.

GENERAL FACILITIES DESIGN CONSIDERATIONS

Certain design considerations apply whether you are planning an audio, audiographic, or video distance learning room. These points are discussed in general terms below; later in this section we will look at the design issues as they relate specifically to rooms for audio, audiographic, and video conferencing.

The distance learning room should be located near the intended users' work areas. It is best to select a room that is convenient for a majority of the intended users. Often there is a tendency to select a location that is particularly convenient for senior managers. If they are expected to be the primary users, such a location may be appropriate, but if the service is going to be shared by middle managers and trainees, you should consider choosing a location away from the executive suite. After all, you do not want to inhibit potential students by creating the impression that the service has been provided exclusively for the executives.

Traffic flow in the area surrounding the selected conference room is an important consideration. Choose a location that is convenient to students, not disruptive of other work operations, and is removed from excessive hallway noise. Because outside noises may also create acoustic difficulties in the conference room, avoid choosing a room with an outside wall that faces a heavily traveled road or other sources of interfering noise.

Room Size.   Room dimensions may vary, but certain proportions enhance the acoustics. The room should meet the needs of the students without being too large or too small. In general, avoid rooms where the ratio of length to width to height is equal or has integral multiples of each dimension, for example, 3:2:1. Thus, a training room approximately 22 ft long, 13 ft wide, and 9 ft high is acceptable and minimizes the amount of reverberation. Ceiling height should be about one-third to two-thirds the width of the room, using the lower ratio for very large rooms and the higher ratio for small rooms. For a room 24 ft by 18 ft, a ceiling height of 10 to 11 ft is optimal.

Room Acoustics.   Both ambient noise and room reverberation must be reduced or eliminated. The acoustic property of the space inside and around the proposed conference room must be evaluated carefully in choosing a location. When people are in the room with the door closed, the room should be almost entirely quiet.

Choosing an interior location in your building will help avoid or minimize outside noise. Attention should be given to both low-frequency noise sources such as elevators, rest rooms, fans, subways, and heavy traffic and high-frequency noise sources such as typewriters, reproduction machines, and public-address systems. If you are near one of these sources of noise, the noise must be blocked.

Within the room, ambient noise and room reverberations (sound bouncing off walls) are the major areas of acoustic concern. Both affect the ability of people in a remote conferencing room to hear what the students in your room are saying.

Ambient noise, or room background noise, must be minimized or eliminated so that distance learning students can hear and be heard easily while they are seated at the conference table. As the room size and the number of people in the room increase, the ambient noise level must be decreased.

Subjective ambient noise testing can be reasonably effective. You can simply enter the room under consideration, close the door, listen for distracting noises, and then determine whether any objectionable noises you hear can be satisfactorily reduced.

The source of ambient noise may be outside the conferencing room. Limiting the effects of external ambient noise depends largely on the source. Noise from outside the building, such as the sounds of aircraft, rail transportation, traffic, and sirens from police or emergency vehicles, can best be limited by selecting an interior room. Noise from mechanical equipment inside the building, such as elevators, fans, compressors, and rest rooms, frequently can be reduced by choosing a location away from the core of the building.

One overlooked source of noise—actually the most frequent offender—is the system used to air-condition the room. Air-conditioning or heater-blower noise should be no more than faintly detectable, yet blower noises are frequently the single largest contributor to the ambient noise in a room. If these noises cannot be corrected by adjusting the equipment, large tapered ducts and slow-speed blowers should be installed. In new rooms this construction should always be specified.

Noise often is generated from general office equipment such as telephone bells, paging systems, reproduction machines, and printers. We recommend that you choose a location well away from these sources of noise. If another room cannot be found and these noise sources cannot be eliminated, you may need to take alternative measures. Windows can be blocked to reduce outside noises. Offset, double-studded, acoustically treated walls can be installed to reduce noise from adjacent rooms. Adjacent corridors can be carpeted to reduce heel-clicking sounds and outside voices.

Noise isolation, which is generally costly and definitely beyond the scope of these guidelines, should be engineered by a qualified acoustic consultant. Acoustic absorption added to lower reverberation in an untreated room will usually decrease the ambient noise:

however, in a noisy environment this small decrease is generally insignificant. If the noise-level requirement cannot be met, you probably will need to select another room location.

One further source of ambient noise is the sounds made by projectors, facsimile machines, and other equipment used in connection with audiographic or video teleconferencing. The proper placement of such equipment can minimize this potential distraction. In addition to removing the offending sources, we recommend that you equip the room with carpeting and padding, an acoustic ceiling, and padded chairs.

Reverberation noise (flutter echo) is sound that bounces off hard walls and echoes around the room. Excessive reverberation or echoing can make it difficult for students to understand what is being said. The quality of the sound transmitted from the room is controlled by the relationship between the microphone and the person who is talking. When the microphone is close to the person speaking, most of the sound that is picked up comes directly from that person; reverberation in the room then exerts relatively little influence. As the distance between the microphone and the person talking increases, however, the direct sound level reaching the microphone decreases quickly, while the average level of the reverberated sound remains constant. As a result, speech becomes less intelligible, of poorer quality, and more tiring to listen to. It acquires a hollowness that makes it sound as if the person were speaking from the bottom of a well.

For good teleconferencing performance, the acoustic properties of the room should prevent flutter echoes between parallel walls and limit room reverberation. The presence of flutter echoes in a room can be detected if you sharply clap your hands and note whether a pronounced echo or reverberation is heard. You can correct such echoes easily by covering adjacent walls with fabric-covered fiberglass acoustic panels 1 to 1.5 in thick. Other ways of dealing with this problem are to use 4-in-thick acoustic foam baffles and freestanding acoustic open-office room dividers set in an L pattern in the room, along adjacent walls. Room "irregularities," such as pillars, window or ceiling recesses, and nonparallel walls, which increase the scattering of sound are also very helpful in reducing reverbertion or echo problems.

Climate Control.   The teleconferencing room should have a comfortable temperature and adequate ventilation. The heating, ventilation, and air-conditioning requirements for a distance learning room are essentially the same as those for a well-designed conventional conference room. Cooling, heating, and air-handling systems should keep the room comfortable while following government energy-conservation guidelines.

The ambient temperature in teleconferencing equipment should be no higher than 80°F, with 50 percent relative humidity. The distance learning room should be zoned separately, with its thermostat located in the room.

You will need to ensure proper ventilation whether or not smoking is permitted in the room, although most distance learning rooms today are designated nonsmoking rooms. The air-moving capacity should be sufficient to avoid the "stuffy" feeling people often perceive when closed in a room. Air also should be circulated through the equipment closet and cabinetry where heat-producing equipment is located.

The distance learning room may be in operation during hours outside the normal business day to communicate with locations in other time zones. For this reason, you may wish to have a separate air-conditioning system for the teleconference facilities so that the company's air-conditioning system can be shut down as usual at the end of the workday.

Lighting and Electrical Power.   Light fixtures, switches, and power outlets should be planned to facilitate programs and presentations. Electrical work includes, but is not limited to, lighting and switching arrangements, power receptacles, conduits for power and telephone service, distribution panels and branch circuitry, smoke detectors, cableways, and wire ways. All electrical work has to be in accordance with national and local codes.

The lighting requirements for an audio or audiographic teleconferencing room are identical to those for a normal conference room. A typical layout might have 2- by 4-ft recessed fluorescent fixtures with four lamps per fixture. The layout should be separated into two or three individually switched circuits to accommodate graphic presentations. This arrangement provides a room illumination range of approximately 30 to 80 foot-candles. The lamps should provide a warm rather than a cool atmosphere, and special quiet ballasts are recommended to eliminate ballast noise.

Room Design.   The appearance and comfort of the conference room affect the way instructors and students feel about distance learning. The colors, fabrics, and furnishings chosen for the teleconferencing room will enhance all the participants' experiences. The conference room should be a comfortable, pleasant place to go with a decor that is somewhat superior to that of the general work areas. The colors selected for interior walls, ceilings, floors, and furnishings should be pleasing in tone and have low reflectance values. The equipment should be unobtrusive so that the users will feel at home and not feel as if they were on stage. Following are recommendations related to specific aspects of the design of a distance learning room.

- *Walls.*   Avoid dark colors; light, neutral tones such as light gold, gray, and brown are more suitable. Fabric-covered acoustic panels may be attached to wall areas for noise reduction. The fabric should be an open-weave, breathe-through material; rubberized material should be avoided.

- *Ceiling.*   An off-white, eggshell-finish acoustic tile suspended ceiling is the best choice for rooms that will be used for teleconferencing.

- *Floor.*   A hard-surface floor should not be used in a teleconferencing room. We recommend covering the floor with a dark, cut-pile, commercial-grade carpet with an undermat. Loop-weave carpet and carpet tiles are also acceptable.

- *Furniture.*   Tables should be light oak, ash, or walnut with a flat or satin finish. Nonreflective plastic laminate is acceptable, but chrome and glass finishes are not recommended. Conference table dimensions should allow each student to have a working area about 29 in wide. The overall size and shape depend on the kind of training for which the room will be used.

- *Chairs.*   Chairs should have upholstered, fabric-covered seats and arms. Avoid the use of chrome, leather, or vinyl. Nonsqueaking swivel, castered tilt chairs with adjustable seats are recommended. The chairs' color should accent the wall and floor colors; however, it is best to avoid very bright, vibrant colors.

- *Windows.*   Although a windowless conference room is preferred, windows can be masked effectively by narrow 1-in-slat venetian blinds with an opaque, lined overdrape. The color scheme should match the walls.

Audio Teleconferencing Room Requirements

It is not necessary to have a dedicated room for audio-only teleconferencing. Well-designed conference rooms are normally very suitable for this type of delivery. In principle, any room is suitable if it is soundproof enough to permit people to converse on high-quality speakerphones. There should be low levels of ambient noise and reverberation. There should be no noticeable voice "clipping" (cutting of speech), and the students should be able to recognize and understand one another easily. If you reserve a room exclusively for audio teleconferencing, the design requirements will be the same as those for the audio component of an audiographic teleconferencing room.

AUDIOGRAPHIC TELECONFERENCING ROOM REQUIREMENTS

The equipment needed for audiographic teleconferencing dictates certain design considerations. For audiographic teleconferencing, a room that is 16 ft by 22 ft with an 8- to 10-ft ceiling will accommodate up to 14 people and meet most training needs. A conference table big enough for 14 people—with 6 along each side and 1 at each end—will fit comfortably in the center of a room this size with space around the perimeter for equipment and additional chairs.

VIDEO TELECONFERENCING ROOM REQUIREMENTS

Rooms used for video teleconferencing generally have location, size, lighting, and furnishing needs different from those of rooms for other communications systems. Below we discuss the desirable characteristics of video teleconferencing rooms.

Room Location.   The video distance learning facility should be in an area that is easily accessible to the greatest number of potential students. Many organizations locate it within the training facility at the origination site. At the receiving sites the video distance learning room is normally a local conference room equipped with portable or roll-about video teleconferencing equipment.

An important factor to consider in deciding on room location is whether you will be offsetting the cost of the video teleconferencing facilities by making them available to other companies or to the public at large when they are not being used by your company. If you expect to resell or share the facilities, you will need to take into account convenience of access by outside users and should plan for a comfortable reception area where students who arrive early can wait for a video teleconference to begin. Lighting in these waiting rooms should be brighter than that in the surrounding office areas but dimmer than that in the video teleconferencing rooms to enable the students to acclimate themselves gradually to the elevated lighting levels in the teleconferencing rooms. If the facilities will be resold or shared, you should provide separate access to these waiting rooms from public areas for both convenience and security reasons. You also should make arrangements to restrict access to the company's general office areas from the video teleconferencing center.

Room Size. The size of a video teleconferencing room is governed by the number of students expected, the amount of equipment, and to some extent camera lens focal length. To avoid the distortion introduced by a wide-angle lens, there must be sufficient distance between the camera and the students to permit the use of a lens of more normal focal length. In the case of an overview camera, this can be a significant consideration, especially when several students are seated along one side of an oval or semicircular table.

Table Size and Shape. The table should be large enough to accommodate comfortably the largest number of students expected to use the video facilities regularly. This number probably will vary from location to location. You may, for example, elect to install 10-position tables at four major corporate locations while using 4- or 6-position tables at locations involving smaller groups. If you intend to resell or share the video teleconferencing facilities, you should take into account the needs of the potential customers in deciding on a table size.

The choice of a table shape is a more complex issue that requires careful consideration of teleconferencing and distance learning applications, group dynamics, user preferences, and space availability. Below are brief descriptions of the options available.

U-shaped table. In this arrangement the students are seated in a pattern that resembles the letter U. The side tables are placed perpendicular to the incoming monitor, with the open end of the U facing that monitor. The table may be in the form of two narrow parallel tables joined at one end, or the center can be filled in, making a single large surface. In contrast to an oval table (see below), the U-shaped configuration tends to direct the attention of the students more to the other people in the room and less to the people at the distant site, a distinction you should consider carefully when making a selection. This arrangement is particularly well suited to programs in which students standing at positions away from the group make presentations that use visual materials. The presenters are able to interact with the people in the room just as they would at an in-person conference.

One disadvantage of this seating arrangement is that some students must turn their heads as much as 180 degrees to look back and forth between the incoming monitor and the other students. Another concern has to do with the placement of the instructor and the location of the document camera. A normal tendency is to seat the instructor at the "head table," that is, at the middle point of the base of the U. If the main camera is placed adjacent to the incoming monitor so that it points down the center of the table, the instructor's image will be the smallest one on the screen. For this reason and because the incoming monitor is less visible from the base of the table in such installations, the instructor is often seated at one of the table ends, closer to the incoming monitor. This gives the instructor a view of remote students and local students as he or she scans the room.

Wedge-shaped table.   This seating arrangement might be described as a U whose arms have been spread apart to allow the students to see the incoming monitor better. The table itself is a single surface in the form of a wedge or, more accurately, an isosceles trapezoid with its wider base near the incoming monitor and parallel to it.

Like a U-shaped table, a wedge-shaped table tends to direct the attention of the students to their fellow students in the same room rather than to the distant locations, although to a lesser extent than does a U-shaped table. The instructor generally is seated at the apex of the table. Depending on the angle of the wedge, the maximum amount of head turning is reduced to under 180 degrees, but it is still considerably greater than is the case when an oval table is used.

Oval table.   An oval table is positioned so that its long axis is parallel to the face of the monitors displaying the incoming pictures. Students are seated along the long side, facing the monitors. The instructor typically sits at the center of the group.

When the oval table arrangement is used with a large-screen video projection, it creates the illusion of a single large conference table, with the students at the distant location occupying the opposite side and each group directing its primary attention to the people at the other location. In this arrangement, when a student's attention alternates between the screen and another local student, a minimum amount of head turning is involved (about 90 degrees at most). This would be the normal amount of head turning in most situations with students in one room seated around a square or rectangular conference table.

A disadvantage of an oval table is that since the students in the two rooms are in effect lined up facing each other, there may be a tendency for an "us versus them" syndrome to develop. The instructor in this situation needs to take particular care to avoid this perception by encouraging interaction among all the students, regardless of their location.

Lighting.   The lighting levels used in a well-lit conference room are adequate for video teleconferencing systems. The exact amount of light you need to provide depends on the requirements of the cameras you select, as specified by the manufacturer. For most equipment, 80 to 100 foot-candles is an adequate level.

Just as important as lighting intensity is the positioning of the lighting fixtures around the room. It is necessary to limit the feeling of being in a television studio so that the students will feel relaxed. You should therefore see to it that lighting fixtures are unobtrusive and, as much as possible, recessed from view. You will also need to plan for the front and back lighting of students to create a realistic three-dimensional effect. This result is much easier to obtain in a room in which the students are seated in a straight line or shallow arc, as they are at an oval table. When students are seated at a U-shaped or wedge-shaped table, providing for both front and back lighting is more difficult since the students are facing in different directions. In such instances track lighting is often appropriate, with several fixtures along the same track aimed in different directions. Track lighting should not look like studio lighting, however; the fixtures should be hidden from view as much as possible, and their design should blend in with the room decor.

Make sure that lights do not cause a glare on the video monitor screens. Glare reduces contrast and is particularly a problem when monitors are used to display documents or graphics, since loss of contrast drastically affects readability.

If you are planning to locate document cameras or other equipment used for presentations away from the main conference table, you will need to provide adequate lighting at those positions as well. Once again, the lighting for these stations must not be permitted to spill onto any of the video monitors in the room.

Finally, remember that the additional heat generated by the lights and equipment required for video teleconferencing must be compensated for when you plan the cooling and air-handling systems of a distance learning room.

INTERNET FACILITIES

Internet-based distance learning systems have minimal facilities requirements. Learners and instructors need a space for their desktop PC, laptop, or notebook computers. The intranet or Internet server usually is housed with the other communications servers in the company's MIS department. You may want to store the information presented on an Internet browser to facilitate larger-group discussion, in which case the design recommendations given for audiographic teleconferencing are appropriate. Specifically, the conference room should be equipped with a large monitor, a video projector or liquid crystal display (LCD) panel, and overhead projector to ensure that all the students see the details of the material projected from the Web pages.

As we stressed in Chap. 4, a distance learning system consists of more than carefully assembled technological delivery media and supporting facilities. The key to the success of a distance learning system is careful attention to the training of instructors and the design and delivery of program content. Chapter 7 offers guidelines for developing distance learning programs that will help you advance your organizational training goals through an effective distance learning program.

FURTHER READING

Chute, A. G. 1990. Strategies for implementing teletraining systems. *Educational and Training Technology International 1990*, 27(3): 264–270.

Chute, A. G., and J. L. Elfrank. 1990. Teletraining: Needs, solutions and benefits. *International Teleconferencing Association Yearbook 1990*, Washington, D.C.: ITCA.

Chute, A. G., M. K. Hulick, C. Messmer, and B. W. Hancock. 1986. Teletraining in the corporate environment. In L. A. Parker and C. H. Olgren (eds.). *Teleconferencing and electronic media*, volume 4, Madison, Wisc.: Center for Interactive Programs.

Hancock, B. W., A. G. Chute, R. R. Raszkowski, and K. M. Austad. 1984. Integration of media components for successful teleconferencing. In L. A. Parker and C. H. Olgren (eds.). *Teleconferencing and interactive media*, Madison, Wisc.: Center for Interactive Programs.

Kester, B. J., T. A. Kester, and A. G. Chute. 1995. Student response systems in corporate distance education. In E. Boschmann (ed.). *The electronic classroom*, Medford, N. J.: Learned Information Inc.

Teleconferencing Managers Guide. 1984. Basking Ridge, N.J.: AT&T Corporation.

PROGRAM DESIGN, DELIVERY, AND EVALUATION

In many organizations the distance learning instructor, often working with a specialized support team, is the key player in the design, delivery, and evaluation of distance learning programs. In other organizations, particularly large ones, design, delivery, and evaluation may be treated as separate functions carried out by individuals in specialized roles. Whether you fill one of the roles or have the responsibility for placing people in those roles, you need a clear understanding of the requirements of the distance learning environment in terms of organizational needs, learning objectives, and instructor skills. Most people who are new to this educational environment need help in finding their distance learning "comfort zone," and that is what we provide in this chapter.

In this chapter we share lessons learned over 25 years of designing and delivering instruction for distance learning environments. We address points to consider in selecting, designing, developing, conducting, and evaluating distance learning programs. We assume that the designers and instructors in your organization are experienced in traditional instruction, and so the intent of this chapter is not to talk about general principles for the development, presentation, or facilitation of educational or training programs. Instead, we focus on the skills these professionals bring to this new environment and describe how to adapt them to the distance learning situation.

Most current distance learning activities are synchronous; that is, they involve students and instructors interacting in real time. For this reason, much of the focus in this chapter is on designing and delivering a synchronous distance learning program. It is increasingly likely, however, that you will be responsible for programs that use asynchronous (delayed-time) approaches, particularly Web-based instruction. Although many of the skills and methods used in designing a synchronous distance learning experience are applicable to Web-based programs, there are some differences. For this reason, this chapter includes a section on the unique instructor skills and methods appropriate for Web-based instruction.

A SYSTEMATIC APPROACH TO THE DESIGN AND DELIVERY OF PROGRAMS

A successful distance learning program must be based on sound program design and effective delivery skills. When a program fails, that is generally due to lack of clarity in program objectives, poor program design, and ineffective instructor delivery skills rather than to the distance learning media. Using a systematic approach to designing programs will help ensure success by providing a step-by-step process that focuses on important elements in the teaching and learning process. This approach to the design and delivery of programs is similar to the process followed in developing other types of training programs, but it pays particular attention to the elements in the process that need to be modified because of the physical separation of the instructor and the learners.

As was noted in Chap. 5, one of the first steps in planning a program is to analyze the particular organizational environment in order to identify performance problems. The identification of performance problems or learning needs is part of a systematic quality improvement program.

The emphasis in educational and training technology has shifted away from classroom instruction and toward a broader view of total job performance. A systematic, bottom-line approach to training is based on a thorough analysis derived from psychological principles of learning and performing. Many major human resource departments use performance improvement and quality improvement standards to analyze current performance, design and develop interventions, select delivery strategies, and conduct follow-up evaluation. The purpose of these activities is to identify and close gaps between desired performance levels and current performance states. However, many performance gaps cannot be addressed solely by means of training interventions. Careful analysis of the environment can avoid the pitfall of prescribing a training solution for a non-training-related problem.

Typically, the performance and task analysis leads to the identification of training needs which either are or can be met by current training strategies, are not being met satisfactorily, or are not being addressed because of various constraints. Needs that are not being met satisfactorily or are not being addressed at all should be the primary focus of intervention efforts.

You will be better able to prescribe distance learning training solutions if you thoroughly understand the systematic approach your training organization uses to determine performance gaps and develop solutions. If a performance problem requires a training solution, you should follow the organization's training development standards in developing the distance learning program.

SELECTING PROGRAMS FOR DISTANCE LEARNING

A frequently asked question relating to distance learning is, What kinds of programs are good candidates for distance learning? In answering this question it is necessary to consider three closely related factors: the business need, the program objectives, and the instructional methods best suited to attaining those objectives.

As was discussed earlier, the decision to use distance learning should be based on the business needs of the organization. Look at the "pressure points" in the organization and identify problems that have training solutions that are not currently being implemented; then determine whether distance learning is a viable means to address those needs. The guiding question should always be, What will distance learning allow me to do that I can't do now? When appropriately applied, distance learning can be a creative solution to many business problems as well as a cost-effective alternative means for the delivery of existing programs.

In our experience, most courses delivered in corporate, government, and higher education programs deal primarily with cognitive (thinking) subject matter and are good candidates for distance learning delivery. Programs with objectives and instructional methods that require a great deal of hands-on practice with special equipment and those which require the evaluation of complex psychomotor skills are generally not good candidates, although some programs of this type—with sufficient resources and excellent course design—have been successfully delivered at a distance. Almost any other type of program can be delivered effectively via distance learning.

IDENTIFYING TEACHING AND LEARNING OBJECTIVES

One of the first and most important steps in the design process is determining the course or program objectives. Once the objectives have been clearly defined, you can select a mode of delivery and instructional methods which are congruent with the objectives. You also will be able to select evaluation measures to determine how well the students have accomplished each objective.

Objectives define the instructional outcomes in terms of what you want the students to know or be able to do as a result of the learning experience. They also identify how subject matter relates to the program as a whole. From the students' perspective, objectives provide a means to identify and focus on key points and offer a framework for studying for tests and evaluations.

Most program objectives fall into one of three classifications: cognitive objectives, which emphasize thinking; affective objectives, which emphasize feeling; and psychomotor objectives, which emphasize kinesthetic activity. Following are examples in each of these categories as they relate to a driver training program.

- *Cognitive objective (knowledge).* On a written test, the applicant will be able to correctly match at least 80 percent of the traffic signs with their descriptions.
- *Affective objective (attitude).* After viewing a film on drunken driving, the applicant will express concern about this social problem and show an interest in learning more about the effect of alcohol consumption on driving capabilities.
- *Psychomotor objective (skill).* During the on-the-road driving test the applicant will perform the required maneuvers at a level satisfactory to the examiner, based on standardized criteria.

Good instructional objectives have clearly stated audiences, behaviors, conditions, and degree phases. This is often called the A-B-C-D approach to writing instructional objectives. *A* is for the learner *audience* that will be performing the task; *B* is for the expected *behavior,* the observable action or task the learner will perform; *C* is for the *conditions* (resources available, time limitations, etc.) under which the audience will perform when being assessed; and *D* is for the *degree* of measurement used to determine an acceptable performance level (for example, 20 out of 20 = mastery; 16 out of 20 is necessary to advance; minimum grade of C, etc.).

Here is an example of a well-written objective: In a role-playing exercise the students will demonstrate four of the five techniques for facilitating group discussion that have been presented in the assigned readings for the class session.

CHOOSING INSTRUCTIONAL METHODS

This phase of the design process matches learning experiences with program objectives. We have found that with a little planning and adaptation, most of the instructional methods commonly used in a traditional face-to-face training environment can be employed successfully in distance learning. Common examples of such methods include lectures, team teaching, celebrity guests, interviews, panel discussions, brainstorming, question-and-answer sessions, reactor panels, buzz groups, group work sessions, role-playing, and case studies. These methods have been described in a number of instructional design textbooks, but special acknowledgment should be accorded to Mavis Monson, author of the popular and still very useful 1976 book *Bridging the Distance*, which describes the incorporation of such methods into the instructional design of a distance learning environment.[1]

The instructional methods listed above also can be categorized in terms of the four types of actions students perform: telling, showing, doing, and evaluating. In our experience in distance learning environments we have used all of these instructional methods; they have worked well for us and should be considered potential starting points as you design your first distance learning programs. Many other combinations are possible, and we encourage experimentation as you become more confident in your distance learning design skills.

INTEGRATING DISTANCE LEARNING TECHNOLOGIES INTO INSTRUCTION

The audio, video, and data distance learning technologies described in Chaps. 2 and 3 often are used as nontraditional vehicles for the delivery of traditional instruction. In other words, these media are used as an alternative means—albeit a cost-effective and education-ally effective one—of presenting information in much the same way it has always been presented: The instructor talks, and the students listen, take notes, and then demonstrate what they have learned on tests or through other evaluative mechanisms.

However, distance learning technologies also can allow instructors to go beyond traditional presentational teaching. The power and flexibility of synchronous and asynchronous communications technologies offer new and enhanced ways to incorporate active and interactive—as well as presentational—learning experiences into distance instruction. By thoughtfully matching the capabilities of technologies with learning objectives and by creatively combining technologies, you can offer students multiple and enhanced channels of communication and a broader repertoire of learning skills and resources.

Technology options that combine voice, data, and video capabilities can convey knowledge and demonstrate skills; they also can support collaborative learning and learning by doing. The discussion that follows focuses on two emerging technology options that have great promise in the distance learning environment: Internet data collaboration and desktop video applications.

INTERNET DATA COLLABORATION

Some managers consider "surfing the Net" one of the all-time great time wasters. However, "browsing the Web," when incorporated into a planned learning experience, can be an effective learning activity. The World Wide Web (WWW) gives both instructors and learners access to resources on thousands of networks worldwide. For these resources to be used effectively in a distance learning program, the instructor must structure the learning activity so that students' browsing activities are focused on processes and content that support the lesson's objectives.

Instructional methods such as case studies and team exercises lend themselves to "Web quests." Teams of students are given questions to answer or a case study that requires follow-up research. Each team may independently browse the Web to locate the needed information. Once the information is found, the team members can get together via live audio or video to share their findings, analyze and synthesize the information, and create what they believe is the appropriate solution. Live audio or video interaction can enable all the teams to share their findings with the entire group. This process is particularly effective in promoting critical thinking and problem-solving skills.

An enhanced feature of some browsers permits groups of students at different locations to browse the same site on the Internet simultaneously. One group can elect to take control of the other locations and point all the browsers to the desired site. In some cases group browsing is coordinated through a simultaneous audio or video teleconference. Voice interaction connects students as they seek and locate. Streaming audio technology soon will make it possible for audio interaction to be carried on the same Internet connection rather than requiring a separate audio teleconference.

Other design options and considerations for Web-based distance learning are discussed later in this chapter.

DESKTOP VIDEO

Many corporate and university personal computer users are adding desktop video software to their computers. With the general availability of the Integrated Services Digital Network (ISDN) and higher-bandwidth services, users in most metropolitan areas can use desktop video as easily as dialing an audioconference call. Desktop video teleconferencing applications make sense when instructors are delivering a distance learning program to small groups of one to three students at remote sites. With desktop video, students and instructors can see and hear each other as they interact in class. Most desktop video software applications also have a feature, referred to as a *share application,* which permits instructors to share with remote students a whiteboard or a software package residing on a desktop personal computer (PC). Software applications for presentations, word processing, and spreadsheets are commonly shared resources.

The share application enables students to collaborate with the instructor and other students as they view and/or revise presentations, reports, graphs, and other types of documents. Instructors also may use this application to display computer graphics and indicate where they want students to annotate pictures or charts. Students can enter and revise data on these documents. When used to support instructional methods such as case studies, brainstorming, and group discussions, desktop video share applications can enhance specific learning goals in a distance learning environment.

GETTING COMFORTABLE WITH DISTANCE LEARNING

Even if you are familiar with developing and delivering educational or training programs in a traditional face-to-face mode, you probably feel apprehensive about trying to use the approaches we have described for training students in multiple sites hundreds of miles away. This feeling is natural for instructors new to the distance learning environment.

In our experience, instructors who are trying something new—moving out of their face-to-face classroom comfort zone—often experience similar anxieties and express common concerns. We have heard the following questions voiced countless times:

- How does the equipment work?
- Will I be able to operate the equipment and teach at the same time?
- Will my students perceive me as a credible instructor?
- How long will it take to learn the skills I need?
- Will students like the program and benefit from it?
- What technologies should I use to be most effective?
- Can I use materials developed for my face-to-face classes?

The first step in adapting to a distance learning environment is to identify your concerns about developing and delivering training programs via distance learning: your personal stress factors. If your concerns have to do with operating distance learning equipment, schedule time to practice with the technology in a low-pressure, nonthreatening situation. Also, talk with other distance learning instructors inside or outside your organization to learn about their experiences. If possible, attend a distance learning program as a student or participate in a workshop that trains instructors to use distance learning equipment. Later in this chapter there is a detailed case study that describes how we developed and delivered a very successful workshop to address these types of concerns.

INSTRUCTOR SKILLS FOR DISTANCE LEARNING

This section discusses design and delivery processes and skills that allow you to set the stage for a distance learning program, adapt face-to-face presentation and facilitation skills to the distance learning environment, and manage the communication process between and among multiple sites. Building on the skills you have while being alert to changes necessitated by the distance learning environment will enhance your effectiveness as a distance learning instructor.

SETTING THE STAGE

First impressions are very important—and lasting. For this reason the instructor needs to set the stage for the distance learning program in the first 20 minutes of the initial session. At this time the students get acquainted with each other, get to know the instructor, and become familiar with the equipment and the protocol they will be using.

An important aspect of setting the stage is identifying everyone's overall expectations of the course. It also helps to anticipate people's concerns about distance learning. It is important to demonstrate the distance learning equipment and give the students an opportunity to try it out.

This initial period provides the foundation for the rest of the program. If the students feel comfortable with each other and the technology, they will be more willing to participate and communicate openly. Following is a job aid for the early establishment of a comfortable distance learning environment.

JOB AID: SETTING THE STAGE	
Opening	*Welcome students to the program:* • Name of program or meeting • Length of program or meeting • Location of each site
Introductions	*Introduce yourself:* • Picture or slide for audio, audiographic, or Internet distance learning • Short biography

Students	*Roll call:* • Acknowledge each individual and test sound quality • Have each student say a few words about himself or herself (site by site) (your introduction should model the pace; keep a meeting roster by location handy)
Coordinator	*Introduce on-site coordinators:* • Give name • Explain purpose • State special tasks or responsibilities • Thank him or her
Expectations	*Discuss expectations:* • Program objectives • Students' expectations of program • Instructor's expectations of students • Elicit, record, and discuss students' concerns
Equipment	*Explain how distance learning is like or not like face-to-face communication:* • Explain or demonstrate equipment • Let students try it out
Administrative items	*Let the students know:* • Courtesy phone numbers for each site • The need for frequent breaks • How you will direct them to media
Distance learning protocol	*Explain the need for special behaviors in distance learning*

An important aspect of setting the stage is giving the students some tips on distance learning protocols. We have found the following "rules of the road" helpful over the years:

- Talk in a normal conversational tone of voice.
- Limit side conversations.
- Avoid paper rustling, tapping, and other distracting noises while the microphones are on.
- Allow ample time for responses. Thinking takes time!
- Synchronize watches and designate a specific time to start the program.
- *Start on time.* It is not fair for other students to have to wait for late-comers.
- Recognize everyone's need to participate actively.

INSTRUCTOR PRESENTATION TECHNIQUES

It is an instructor's responsibility to deliver information to the group in such a way that it will be received, understood, and remembered. In synchronous distance learning, where students receive a large proportion of the information through listening, messages should be designed for the ear as much as possible. Communication is enhanced through the use of various vocal, listening, and interactive techniques. This section describes ways to incorporate these techniques into an instructor's delivery style.

Vocal Techniques.   Just as important as *what* you say is *how* you say it. Your voice can reflect interest or apathy, confidence or uncertainty, emphasis or anticipation.

The following vocal techniques are important in a distance learning environment. Varying one's voice quality and rate of speech can greatly enhance the effectiveness of a program or meeting. Good vocal techniques are critical in an environment as listening-dependent as a distance learning setting. Following are some tips on different aspects of vocal delivery:

- *Pitch* (the highness or lowness of a voice, based on the frequency of the sound produced). Pitch should be neither too high nor too low and should be varied to prevent monotony.
- *Volume* (the intensity or force with which a voice is projected). It is not necessary to scream to compensate for the distance in distance

learning. Vary your volume to illustrate a point or show emphasis but never speak so softly that the listener has to strain to hear you.

- *Enunciation* (the way words are articulated). Mumbling causes frustration on the part of the listener; if the message is not received clearly, the students may turn off to the class or meeting. Remember that the English language is full of similar sounds (T and D, P and B, etc.); clear enunciation helps prevent misunderstandings and the need to repeat.

- *Pacing* (the rate of speech). Speaking too slowly causes boredom and irritation; speaking too quickly may prevent the students from understanding the information you are trying to communicate. Vary the speed in accordance with the message; for example, slowly introduce a new topic, more quickly review previous material, pause to draw attention to an important topic, and regularly insert a 7- to 10-second break before proceeding to allow students to ask questions or make comments.

- *Enthusiasm* (readily apparent interest in the subject matter). The instructor's level of enthusiasm conveys his or her interest in the topic to the students and often enhances their interest and motivation.

Two other vocal techniques or qualities that can be employed to ensure an effective presentation are summary and repetition. A summary that reviews the main points aids retention, as does grouping key points in clusters or chunks. Research in the cognitive sciences suggests that cluster sizes of seven (plus or minus two) points are the most effective in facilitating students' retention and learning. Repetition is another helpful aid to memory. After teaching a new fact or concept, repeat it several times during the subsequent presentation to help the students remember it.

Facilitating Effective Listening.   Another important factor is listener fatigue. Although listener attention is usually high at the beginning of a program, it often levels off in the middle and then increases again as the students perceive that the program is coming to a close. For this reason, incorporating messages into the main body of the presentation that will stimulate the audience and keep its attention and retention levels high is an effective instructional technique.

In distance learning situations, the instructor should vary the message style or medium approximately every 20 minutes. Variety keeps interest levels high and leads to more active listening. The following tips help minimize listener fatigue:

- Keep messages short and to the point. Limit the number of key points presented in each segment to seven (plus or minus two).
- Begin the lesson or meeting with an outline or description of its structure and activities.
- Give the students a "listening break" every 15 to 20 minutes.
- Insert into the presentation listening cues such as "This is important..." and "Now, remember this...."
- Paraphrase complex questions.
- Make a mental or written note of student responses for later reference.
- Use repetition and summary as a way to emphasize key points and aid retention.

An instructor also must be a good listener. Just as the instructor's tone of voice and inflections convey messages to the students, the tone of students' remarks and questions can give an instructor who listens carefully clues to their mood and attitude. If you are using a video system, nod your head to acknowledge that you have heard their comments.

Personalizing Techniques.   Most learning experiences are enhanced by interaction, especially in distance learning situations, where the physical distance between the instructor and the students at various sites may be perceived as a psychological barrier to communication. You can make the medium being used transparent and user-friendly by promoting student-student and student-instructor interaction. "Personalizing" the program will make students feel more closely involved and make the distance learning experience richer and more satisfying for them.

Personalizing is an instructional technique used to create an atmosphere of group rapport and individual inclusion. The process of getting to know one another is an important step in the teaching and learning process. The instructor must recognize the uniqueness of each student but at the same time point out common backgrounds and interests among the members of the group. Through personalizing students increase their knowledge of the instructor and of each other. As a result, they feel more comfortable in sharing their ideas and are more confident that their individual needs will be met. There is a direct relationship between personalizing, participation, and satisfaction. Following are some suggestions for personalizing instruction.

- Send students a course outline, a welcome letter, and an instructor biography before the course or training session begins.
- If possible, make a preprogram telephone call to the students to find out about their backgrounds.
- Distribute to all the students a master roster that includes each student's name, title, location, telephone number, fax number, video number, and E-mail address.
- Point out areas of common interests to allow the group members to identify more closely with one another.
- Open each session with an informal roll call.
- Encourage the students to describe their expectations.
- Always call the students by name.

Personally follow up on all questions.

Following is an example of a welcome letter and an instructor biography sent to students in a distance learning course.

SAMPLE WELCOME LETTER

On behalf of the Center for Excellence in Distance Learning, I am confirming your reservation to attend the distance learning skills seminar.	Program name
Date: _____ to _____ Time: _____ to _____	Program date and time
Location: _____ _____ _____	Class location
The seminar is designed to provide you with the necessary skills and knowledge to effectively make presentations and conduct meetings in a distance learning environment.	Program objectives
The learning experience will be greatly enhanced by your active participation; therefore, please bring to class a presentation you have	Precourse or other special requirements

worked on to use during the class exercises. You will actually prepare a presentation and deliver a 20- to 30-minute distance learning program to the rest of the class using distance learning technology.

Precourse or other special requirements

If the program is not being received at your work location, the travel and lodging arrangements will be your responsibility. Return travel reservations can be made for (date) after 3 p.m.

Travel information

The Center for Excellence in Distance Learning staff is looking forward to meeting with you on (date). If you need assistance in securing lodging or if you have any other questions, please feel free to contact us at (phone number).

Welcome paragraph and contact member

SAMPLE INSTRUCTOR BIOGRAPHY

Alan G. Chute, Ph.D.
Chief Learning Strategist
Lucent Technologies: Bell Labs Innovations
Call Center Institute and Center for Excellence in Distance Learning
Cincinnati, Ohio

"I like to manage projects from the ground up," says Alan Chute. "I enjoy starting from scratch and building systems of people, places, and technology."

For the past 25 years Alan has had ample opportunity to do just that! Alan established the AT&T National Teletraining Center and the AT&T Teletraining Networks, which won the 10-Year Distinguished Service to the Industry Award from the United States Distance Learning Association. In 1994 Alan was elected to the Hall of Fame of the International Teleconferencing Association. He was the AT&T project director for the Indiana University Center for Excellence in Education, a national demonstration center for the future of technology in education. He has also been a university professor and the director of a statewide medical distance learning system.

Alan was an officer with the U.S. Army Signal Corps in Europe and holds a B.S. degree in mathematics and M.S. and Ph.D. degrees in instructional technology from the University of Wisconsin. He has published over 50 articles and books on a diverse range of subjects, including advanced learning systems, reengineering of training organizations, and the future of distance learning.

Alan currently directs the Lucent Technologies Call Center Institute (CCI) and the Center for Excellence in Distance Learning (CEDL). The mission of the CCI is to enhance the knowledge and skills of professionals in the call center discipline. CEDL's overall mission is to advance the state of the art in distance learning applications and technologies.

For more information visit the Center for Excellence in Distance Learning at www.lucent.com/cedl and the Call Center Institute at www.lucent.com/cci.

Questioning Techniques. Questioning is another technique that allows an instructor to actively involve students in the teaching and learning process. Questions not only encourage group members to contribute, they also prompt them to interact with the content: the instructor's words, the text, or the visual materials in front of them.

Question-and-answer interactions are at the core of effective instructional communications. They are especially important in a distance learning environment and accomplish several goals:

- Determining whether the students understand and accept the information the instructor is giving them
- Reviewing the material presented previously
- Facilitating understanding and gaining a consensus
- Managing student behavior

Asking effective questions encourages participation and interaction among students and sites. Questions can range from those focusing on simple recall of knowledge, comprehension of concepts, and application of rules to those prompting complex levels of thought that require analysis, synthesis, and evaluation. Questions play an integral role in the communication process, and the effectiveness of an instructor is enhanced greatly by good questioning techniques and skills. Three types of questions—directed questions, redirected questions, and rhetorical questions—are effective in promoting interaction in a distance learning environment and should be incorporated into an instructor's delivery style.

Questions directed to a specific student or location generally stimulate a response, since the participants who are singled out feel an obligation to respond. By preparing students for this directed question approach at the beginning of an activity, you can create a less threatening atmosphere. The best strategy is to ask the question, direct it to a location, and then direct it to a student. Using this procedure will encourage all students—rather than just the person or site named—to listen to the question and think about an answer.

Redirecting student questions to other students is an extremely effective method of generating student involvement and interaction in educational activities. Frequent use of this technique will encourage students to ask each other questions or offer comments, overcoming their tendency to direct all questions or comments to the instructor. Such student-student interaction lessens the psychological distance that can exist between geographically separated students.

Rhetorical questions—those to which one does not expect an answer—can stimulate student thinking. Consider asking a question that you suspect the students are thinking about and then answering that question yourself. This technique is especially effective in making presentations to large groups because it covertly stimulates participation and can be used as a natural transition between concepts. It is also useful when an instructor wants to encourage students to consider perspectives that may not have occurred to them.

Based on our years of experience in designing and delivering distance learning instruction, we offer the following tips and techniques for effective questioning in the distance learning environment.

- *Plan key questions to provide direction to the program content.* Ask at least one question to promote higher-order thinking: application, analysis, or evaluation. Ask spontaneous questions based on students' responses and ask questions logically and sequentially.

- *Phrase questions clearly and specifically.* Avoid vague, ambiguous questions. Ask questions one at a time; avoid run-on questions that lead to frustration and confusion. Remember that clarity increases the probability of getting accurate responses.

- *Adapt questions to the students' ability level.* Use appropriate-level questions to enhance understanding and reduce anxiety and boredom. Adjust your vocabulary and sentence structure to the students' language and conceptual levels. Use knowledge-level questions to determine basic understanding and higher-level questions to stimulate and challenge students.

- *Follow up on students' responses.*   Encourage students to clarify, expand, or support their responses. Ask other sites for additional input: Can you clarify that further? What are some alternatives? Can you add anything more?

- *Give students sufficient time to respond.*   Allowing sufficient time to ensure student understanding encourages higher-level thinking.

- *Use questions that encourage wide participation.*   Ask questions that involve a majority of the students and encourage intersite and intrasite interaction. Involve reticent students through directed questions.

- *Encourage students to ask questions.*   Develop a supportive climate to encourage participation and interaction by accepting and applying students' ideas, using positive reinforcement, and responding to students' feelings.

- *Track students' responses.*   To keep track of students' responses, make a chart that groups students by site:

Atlanta	*Chicago*	*Denver*	*Seattle*
Alan	Brenda	Carol	Barb
Herb	Burton	Katie	Keith
Pam	Hillary	Matt	Melody
Richard	Meredith	Megan	Tom

If you record the students' responses on the chart, you can then direct questions toward those students with fewer check marks to involve them in the discussion and activities.

MEDIA UTILIZATION TECHNIQUES

The most important channel of communication in synchronous distance learning is the audio channel. Although the participants may be willing to put up with less than optimal video or graphic quality, they invariably demand high-quality audio communication. For this reason, any media or technologies you use must serve as a reinforcement of the audio message, not as a distraction. Adding media (on-camera video, videotapes, handouts, three-dimensional object media, and computer graphics) to a distance learning program should enhance what the listeners hear by activating and stimulating other senses.

You will need to establish a careful and dynamic relationship between the audio and the visual media you employ. At times the audio channel may have to be silenced to allow time for the eye to undistractedly record the visual message. At other times a computer graphic can enhance an audio presentation by cueing the appropriate human sensory channel. Whatever media are used, their relationship must be mutually reinforcing. Print material can reinforce what students hear and serves as a permanent record for review.

Here are some tips on media utilization:

- Concentrated listening should be limited to short segments.
- Variety in media helps keep the interest level high.
- Media can be used to stimulate individuals to interact with what is being presented.
- Print materials can be used to support the lecture or presentation. Print provides a second way to get the message across and serves as a permanent record or reviewing device.
- It is a good idea to limit the amount of notes the students have to take in a videoconferencing environment. Time spent in note taking usually is better spent listening and thinking.

PRESENTATION FORMAT

In designing and delivering a distance learning program, you should organize the content into a preview-present-review format. In other words, you should first tell the students what you are going to talk about, then talk about it, and finally summarize what you have told them.

Previewing the session at the beginning informs students about the scope of the session and describes how the content material is relevant to them. Specifically, the preview should address the importance of the topic to the audience, the objectives of the program, the structure of the presentation, and any expectations the instructor has of the students.

In the present portion of a distance learning program, you deliver the content material in such a way that it facilitates understanding and encourages participation. This portion also includes a description of the presentation methods, the media utilization techniques, and the interaction strategies the instructor and students will use.

At the conclusion of a session, key points are reviewed to reinforce understanding and stimulate retention. The review includes a recap of key points, student feedback, and a closing statement or transition to the topic that will be discussed in the next session.

Visual Support Materials. It is the instructor's responsibility to ensure that all the visuals used in the presentation conform to guidelines for transmission clarity. Some of these visuals, such as the course outline or agenda, will be distributed before presentations, while others are suitable as presentation or postmeeting reference materials (for example, evaluation forms, copies of computer graphics, policy documents).

Charts, graphs, text slides, and diagrams suitable for printing may not be suitable for visual display on a monitor in audiographic conferencing or videoconferencing. They may include large amounts of information and be acceptable in a printed report or a manual, but those formats permit detailed, close-up study, which usually is not possible with projected materials. However, they may work fine in Internet delivery because the students usually can control the image size and font size through their local Web browsers.

In designing the instruction, try to limit yourself to the presentation of one idea at a time. To do this, you can employ specific visual tools (line, shape, space, texture, and color), certain design principles (simplicity, emphasis, balance, and unity), and guidelines for quality, proportion, and size. Consider the following tips for preparing visual materials for distance learning.

- Visual pages, slides, or frames should be three units high by four units wide (i.e., the aspect ratio of the television or computer display monitor).

- The textual content for visuals should be limited to fewer than 25 words. The type size for transmitted images should be at least 28 points. The text should be limited to no more than 40 characters (including spaces) on a single line and no more than 10 lines per page.

- Sanserif and gothic type styles are easy to read. Avoid script styles because they are more difficult to read. Limit the number of different styles in the same visual or series of visuals.

- Generally speaking, the fewer elements into which a given space is divided, the more pleasing it is to the eye.

- Lengthy or complex data should be subdivided or redesigned into a series of easy-to-read and easy-to-understand related materials.

- A line in a visual can connect the elements and direct the viewer to study the elements in a specific sequence. Plan visual materials so that the lines are already drawn or use the graphics tablet to annotate, adding visual interest and variety to the program.

- Unusual shapes, textures, and colors give special interest to a visual or emphasize an element within a visual.

- Open space around visual elements and words will prevent a crowded feeling and provide an area for annotation.

- Text can be combined with pictures to attain an asymmetrical balance that makes visuals more dynamic and attention-getting.

Visual clarity also is related to viewing distance. For television monitors, the standard maximum acceptable distance is eight times the horizontal dimension of the viewing screen (i.e., eight times the width, or 8W). Thus, for a screen that is 2 ft (24 in) wide, the maximum viewing distance is 8×2, or 16 ft. For large audiences in spacious auditoriums, the image on the television monitor may have to be projected on a larger viewing screen.

PRESENTATION SKILLS

The facilitation and platform skills you have used in presentations and face-to-face educational programs—providing information, interacting with the audience, and varying the message style—are especially important in distance learning programs. These skills need to be adapted and given special attention in those programs to compensate for the physical distance between instructors and their audiences.

On-Camera Skills. The effective use of the visual channel in video teleconferencing instruction requires attention to several factors. As with any new skill, an instructor can improve more quickly with mentoring and lots of practice. Look for opportunities to observe experienced instructors and, if possible, codeliver distance learning programs with them. Unfortunately, not everyone has the opportunity to work with an experienced mentor; a trial-and-error approach may be the one you have to follow. Following are some considerations in developing delivery skills for the video teleconferencing medium. By following these guidelines, you will be able to present a more professional image on camera.

Camera Considerations. The cameras should be adjusted to preset positions to maintain screen balance, that is, with an equal space on either side of the subject. Examine the screen edge of each preset shot for distractions; do not consider only the center portion of the screen. The instructor or room coordinator should frame the preferred camera shots in advance. Today most cameras with pan, tilt, and zoom mechanisms allow a user to preset at least four camera positions which can be recalled with the press of a button.

As in face-to-face programs, maintain eye contact, but now with the camera. Looking down or away gives the appearance of lack of attention or impersonality. As in face-to-face communication, active listening and eye contact are crucial. Use body language—nodding, pointing, and the like—instead of voice to exhibit understanding or signal others. (However, if you are instructing via compressed video or another system that entails a time delay of a few seconds in the transmission of your image, remember that broad, sweeping gestures will be blurred and therefore distracting for viewers at distant sites.)

You should avoid harsh, direct light such as desk lamps and direct sun. Harsh lights create "hot spots" and shadows; these extremes of contrast may exceed the range of the video camera and cause detail to be lost in whiteout or gray areas. Try to produce an even, soft light.

Backgrounds should be neutral in tone. Avoid very bright or dark backgrounds. Also, keep the person who is the focus of attention away from backgrounds so that shadows do not become a problem. Make sure that items such as plants, picture frames, and window edges do not appear to "grow" out of the person on camera.

Video Presentation Considerations. To appear organized during video instruction and to minimize visual distractions, make sure you have everything set up before the beginning of a session. Arrange all video source material and user control functions so that they are readily accessible and easy to use. In fact, we recommend that new distance learning instructors come into the room at least a half hour before the session begins to get comfortable and make sure everything is ready to go. We often encourage instructors to go out of the room and take a short break before the program starts. Get some coffee or a soft drink, stop at the rest room, or read the headlines in the newspaper to relax.

Careful selection and positioning of equipment coupled with a proper setup of the videoconferencing room will result in optimal system performance. Position microphones to allow students to speak without raising their voices and listen without straining. Instruct the students to adjust the incoming volume controls to set up a comfortable listening level. The students at each receiving site should mute their microphones when not speaking. Inform the students of the relevant protocols for the program; have the receiving sites numbered and let everyone know who is where and in what order the sites will respond and interact.

Use monitors large enough to enable students to read materials on the screen without straining. The size of the monitor depends on the size of the room. Students in the front of the room should be no closer than two times the width of the video monitor, and students in the back should be no farther away than eight times the width of the monitor.

Above all, be yourself! Let your personality, normal presentation style, and charisma come through. Relax and capitalize on your strengths, and you will be successful.

CONTINGENCY PLANS

Some first-time instructors feel a loss of control as they think about what it will be like to teach students at a distance. The best advice we can give you is to practice delivering the beginning module and develop a set of contingency plans for what to do if something does not go the way you expect it to. If you have a plan, you will feel more in control. Some of the most common concerns expressed by new distance learning instructors begin with the words "What do I do if…?"

The key to any successful program is plenty of up-front planning, especially in the distance learning environment, where instructors must coordinate multiple sites in addition to overseeing routine program logistics. The next section details preventive measures that will minimize the possibility of problems occurring in the first place. Those suggestions are followed by job aid that offers solutions to several "what if" questions.

- *Handling materials.*   Mail materials out as far in advance as possible to allow time for subsequent mailings if the original mailing is delayed or lost.

- *Testing equipment.*   The best way to prevent the malfunctioning of equipment during an instructional session is to check everything beforehand both at your site and at the remote sites. The on-site coordinator for each site will have to troubleshoot problems that arise at the remote end, so make sure he or she is familiar with the equipment.

- *Handling distracting student behavior.* Consideration for others and courtesy over the distance learning medium are very important. Time spent at the beginning of the program laying out the ground rules is time well spent. As the instructor, you need to encourage as much interaction as possible, but at times you may need to interrupt or control side conversations and multiple speakers. The best method to make sure all sites are paying attention and following the lesson is to use the strategy of directed and redirected questions that was discussed earlier.

JOB AID: CONTINGENCY PLANS	
Materials do not arrive	Send out student materials early to each remote location and verify their receipt two days before the program.
	Give yourself enough lead time to be able to use an express mail service or fax if the materials were not received at the remote locations.
	Test equipment before class.
Equipment malfunctions	Exchange emergency phone numbers with each remote site.
	Know what backup systems are available and be able to talk the site coordinator through setup procedures.
	Create a learning experience for students by explaining troubleshooting procedures.
	Use the site coordinator as your eyes at the remote sites to identify potential problems before they surface.

Difficult students	Try to handle students' objections during the program and turn them into learning experiences.
	Discuss students' problems with the site coordinator on the courtesy phone during a break.

DESIGN CONSIDERATIONS FOR WEB-BASED LEARNING

Web-based distance learning solutions give learners access to the training and information they need *at a time and place convenient for them*. The Web-based learning experience can include live synchronous training components, self-paced learning activities, and/or asynchronous interactions with instructors and other learners. The design elements and processes of Web-based educational or training materials closely parallel those of good synchronous distance learning programs, as described earlier in this chapter. The key difference is that the various instructional methods you select to stimulate participation and create a sense of community among the learners will result in learner interactions that occur in somewhat different ways and at different times in the instructional sequence.

For example, using the question-and-answer instructional method will prompt learners to react to your questions as well as the comments of other learners just as they do in synchronous contexts. However, the learners will be reading the questions on computer screens and typing in their answers on keyboards. These interactions are likely to occur over a period of several days or weeks rather than in the scheduled 15-minute question-and-answer period you might plan for a synchronous distance learning session.

We have found that asynchronous learner interactions via E-mail or Web-based discussion forums often encourage higher levels of thought than do the spontaneous discussions that take place in typical audio or video distance learning courses or face-to-face instruction. Using thought-provoking questions that require analysis, synthesis, or evaluation of the content areas being discussed is appropriate, since learners in this environment have more time to reflect on their answers. Often learners in Web-based classes take more care with their answers than do those in a spontaneous synchronous discussion; the act of putting their ideas in writing encourages them to put their best thoughts forward, since those thoughts become part of a permanent or semipermanent class record.

Web-based learning offers other benefits as well. Learners who speak English as a second language often prefer asynchronous participation in discussions because they have time to reflect on questions and carefully compose their responses and because their written English is usually better than their spoken English. Asynchronous question-and-answer sessions or discussions also permit the instructor to monitor participation more closely and encourage all the learners to participate, which can be difficult in a class with a rigid time frame or large numbers of learners. Another benefit of Web-based interaction is that an intellectually stimulating discussion that takes place in one class can "persist" in cyberspace indefinitely. Learners can access a prior class's discussions and continue a discussion thread through interactions with their current classmates.

Other teaching methods can be incorporated into the course design. With modifications that take into account the time-delayed and text-based nature of most Web-based distance learning, interviews, panel discussions, brainstorming, role-playing, case studies, and other instructional methods discussed in this chapter can be used effectively in this environment. All these methods can help the instructor realize general teaching objectives such as promoting learner understanding and stimulating critical thinking about the concepts presented in the course.

One tool that can help an instructor implement a Web-based distance learning solution that allows for synchronous and/or asynchronous interaction is the Persyst suite of software tools developed by Lucent Technologies' Bell Labs. This rich multimedia environment uses the Internet, the World Wide Web, corporate intranets, and local area networks (LANs) to deliver instruction. By using the image of the classroom as the instructor-learner visual interface, this virtual classroom environment offers all the necessary "spaces" required for the rich, interactive delivery of learning materials.

The instructor can design for real-time lectures, digitally "taped" delayed-time lectures and other audio presentations, customized libraries and archives with learner materials for case studies, work spaces for learner work group collaboration and role-playing, and virtual "theaters" for watching and hearing audio or video materials. The instructor can incorporate a variety of methods into the design of other virtual spaces to meet instructional, learner, and content needs. Additional tools include a group calendar and individual calendars for classes, instructors, and learners to permit the scheduling of interactions, E-mail utilities, facilitated and nonfacilitated chat spaces, learner log-in monitoring, testing and automated scoring and response database creation, and other functions required to complete the learning environment.

The Persyst virtual classroom is accessible to a learner site (e.g., office, home, or training facility) equipped with a PC, a Web browser, Internet access through a modem or private network, a sound card, and readily attainable "freeware" plug-ins. The virtual classroom is intended for use over intranets, the Internet, or LANs, as depicted in Fig. 7-1.

Another tool for designing Web-based instruction is WebCT, a suite of World Wide Web course tools (hence the "CT"). WebCT features tools that allow nontechnical users, both instructors and students, to participate fully in the on-line learning environment. For the instructor, WebCT offers tools for designing progress tracking; timed, on-line, automatically graded quizzes; student management (class lists, grades, etc.); access control; course backup and transfer; a course welcome page; and more. Students communicate and learn with tools that include a searchable course conferencing system (bulletin board) for interaction with the instructor and other students, one-to-one electronic mail, chat rooms for synchronous communication, self-evaluations, a searchable image archive and glossary, a student presentation area, links to external references, a study guide generation tool, and a student home page tool.

Required hardware and software for operation are minimal: A networked computer and a Web browser (for example, Netscape 2.0 or higher) are all that's needed to access a WebCT server to create and/or modify a course, grade students' work, or learn. In most cases the WebCT server is installed and maintained by the course developer

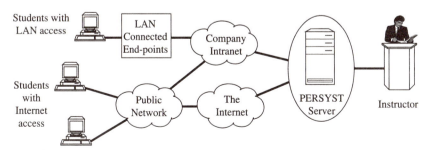

FIGURE 7-1.   The Persyst virtual classroom.

or by the network administrator at the developer's institution or organization. Some Internet Service Providers (ISPs) also provide access to WebCT.

For now, the computer that runs the WebCT server must run the UNIX operating system; however, the developers of this product are currently testing a Windows version. A single WebCT server can support the development and delivery of many courses. You can download WebCT free from the Web and try it out in the design of Web-based courses. License fees apply only when a course is made available to students. More information about obtaining and using WebCT is available from the WebCT home page (http://homebrew.cs.ubc.ca/webct/).

The WWW offers instructors a rich and varied framework within which to design multimedia distance learning programs that are within easy reach of learners around the corner or around the world. Because Web-based distance learning builds on existing assets—the computers used by the employees and the organization's established network for Internet or intranet access—it provides a convenient and flexible way to reach learners.

HELPING OTHERS GET COMFORTABLE WITH DISTANCE LEARNING

An instructor learning the ins and outs of design and delivery for distance teaching can count on one thing: Just about the time the instructor begins to get his or her bearings, to feel a level of comfort with the idea and practice of distance learning, others in the organization will begin to look to that instructor as *the* distance learning expert. Even though you may not feel like an expert yet, you probably are going to have to help beginning instructors—not to mention the students—find their own comfort zones. Alternatively, you may not be an instructor but may be charged with the training or retraining of instructors in using a new distance learning system. Providing direction and support for those new to the distance learning environment is an important aspect of the overall program design.

One of the critical steps in the implementation of a distance learning system is to get people to use and support the new system. As was discussed in Chap. 5, there is a well-recognized change process that people go through in adjusting to any innovation, and the change roles and processes throughout the organization as they relate to distance learning also were discussed. This section will revisit some to the concepts that were introduced earlier and focus on the process of helping others progress from novices to beginners to experienced instructors and users.

The first step in this aspect of the change process is to assess the needs of instructors, on-site coordinators, and students and identify their concerns regarding distance learning. The instructor then needs to prescribe interventions such as training workshops and mentoring activities that will address those expressed needs and concerns.

The detailed case study later in this chapter explains how a member of our group successfully facilitated the change process for a medical school as it implemented a statewide medical distance learning system. In this case, as is generally the case with the introduction of an innovative distance learning system, there was a period of cautiousness—a trial stage—before the innovation was adopted by and integrated into the organization. We believe that the level of instructor, on-site coordinator, and student acceptance of the distance learning innovation depend on the degree to which each individual's needs are addressed. As you implement a distance learning system, you will have to determine and communicate the relationship between these needs and the ability of the innovation to meet them.

HELPING NEW INSTRUCTORS ADAPT

Innovation can be a powerful force for renewal in organizations. To make it work, it is necessary to understand the motivations of the individuals who are going through the change process.

Rogers and Shoemaker offered the following definition of the term *innovation*:

> An innovation is an idea, practice, or object perceived as new by an individual. It matters little, so far as human behavior is concerned, whether or not an idea is "objectively" new as measured by the lapse of time since its first use or discovery. It is the perceived or subjective newness of the idea for the individual that determines his reaction to it. If the idea seems new to the individual, it is an innovation (p. 19).[2]

To bring about the adoption of distance learning as a viable instructional method, the first step is to assess the needs of the instructors who will be involved. Those needs must be understood and addressed if the change strategy to be effective. As Eraut states:

> Unless an educator perceives some discrepancy between his goals and his achievements, he is bound to regard innovation as undesirable and unnecessary; and the extent to which his expressed dissatisfaction is fundamental or trivial will determine the extent to which he is likely to entertain innovation. If an educator does not have a problem, innovation will seem irrelevant (p. 14).[3]

Typically, individuals in the process of change express a variety of concerns that indicate their feeling toward the innovation. According to Hall,[4] those involved in the adoption of an innovative program or project exhibit seven levels or stages of concern: awareness, information, personal, management, consequence, collaboration, and refocusing. First people become aware that there is a new approach. They then actively seek information about it. After they come to understand the information, they have personal reactions to it and actively seek ways to manage it. When they have considered the consequences of the innovation for their students, they next look for ways to collaborate with others to develop a deeper understanding of the innovation. Finally, they refocus their attention on the universal benefits and impact of the innovation on the organization as a whole.

Instructors involved in the process of adopting an innovation may express concerns which fall within several of Hall's stages; that is, a profile reflecting several different levels of concern can be observed in each individual involved. Over time, the profile will change, indicating that the individual has progressed from lower-level informational concerns to personal concerns to impact-level concerns.

Research by Hall and others led to the development of the Concerns Based Adoption Model (CBAM),[5] which you can use to develop the questionnaires and interviews you will need to assess the changes in the levels of concern expressed by the instructors, the on-site coordinators, and the students with whom you are working. Additionally, the model can be used as a guide to the choice of intervention strategies—such as staff development workshops—that will hasten the acceptance of an innovation.

The CBAM also provides a step-by-step guide to the types of concerns you are likely to encounter as you progress through the change process. For example, we have found that new instructors want to obtain information on how the equipment works and its reliability. They wonder how well they personally will do in the distance learning environment. They are concerned about mastering distance learning "classroom" management so that they can appear professional in their particular delivery media. Later they probably will want to collaborate with peers in affinity groups to refine their skills further. The model clearly articulates these progressive concerns and provides a framework for designing and scheduling interventions to appropriately match current stages of concern. The CBAM thus functions as a valuable diagnostic and prescriptive tool in the distance learning change process.

CASE STUDY: A WORKSHOP ON THE ADOPTION OF A DISTANCE LEARNING SYSTEM[6]

This case study describes the strategy we used at the South Dakota Medical Information Exchange (SDMIX) to implement a statewide medical distance learning system in the 1980s. Since then, the School of Medicine has successfully used its distance learning system to deliver hundreds of continuing and graduate-level medical education programs, Category One American Medical Association (AMA) continuing education units, and nursing education programs. This case study also explains how we applied the principles of change theory and concern theory in a series of distance learning workshops for medical school faculty and staff.

One of the first steps was to identify the concerns of the faculty regarding the innovation through questionnaires and interviews. From their responses we identified two major concerns: Can distance learning be an effective medium for the delivery of high-quality medical instruction? and Can faculty members who are unfamiliar with the technological and program aspects of distance learning use the medium effectively?

To facilitate organizational acceptance of the innovation—an audio distance learning system—we assumed the role of change agent. We worked closely with the SDMIX staff to address the needs and concerns of the distance learning faculty by conducting workshops and providing mentoring for distance learning instructors. Our goal was to address users' concerns regarding the system and foster enthusiasm for the acquisition of new presentation skills. We knew that neglecting to change attitudes while we were improving skill levels probably would result in faculty frustration and rejection of the innovation.

In the workshop we separated faculty members into small groups, allowed them to experiment with the distance learning equipment, and assisted them as they began to design their own 15-minute trial program. Faculty members were given hands-on experience in setting up the distance learning equipment, dialing into the audio bridge, and interacting with other locations using the distance learning system. These experiences reduced their concerns about the distance learning technology and thus increased the probability that they would adopt this innovation. This segment of the workshop was intended to create a positive attitude toward the distance learning medium.

After the faculty members and staff became comfortable with the hardware, we shifted the focus of the workshop to program design. The next steps included identification of the content area, the intended audience, and the goals and objectives of the presentation. The SDMIX staff assisted the group in narrowing the topic to fit a 15-minute time period, developing a content outline, specifying support materials, and planning strategies to encourage interaction. We then worked with the faculty to establish the criteria for evaluation and develop an instrument and/or procedure to assess whether the criteria had been met.

This workshop, which was designed to address the needs and concerns of the faculty, was based on a plan derived from the change model of Havelock[7] and the CBA model of Hall.[8] The five-stage SDMIX workshop plan had the following components:

1. Determining presenters' needs and concerns
2. Creating awareness of and interest in distance learning
3. Providing information about distance learning
4. Teaching distance learning techniques
5. Changing presenters' attitudes and behaviors

DETERMINING PRESENTERS' NEEDS AND CONCERNS

As was mentioned earlier, we used interviews and questionnaires to assess the needs and concerns of the faculty. Frequently expressed concerns involved instructional effectiveness and the technical capabilities of distance learning. These concerns were manifested in statements such as the following:

1. It is not as good as face-to-face instruction.

2. People don't understand what is being taught.
3. The equipment might break down.
4. I sense a lack of control.
5. How much can I effectively cover during a distance learning program?
6. Distance learning is not spontaneous.
7. Is my presentation good enough for distance learning?

We developed and delivered various presentation segments and learning activities within the workshop to address each of these concerns.

CREATING AWARENESS OF AND INTEREST IN DISTANCE LEARNING

We knew that although some of the potential users already might have been exposed to the concept of distance learning, they probably had not learned enough about it to form lasting opinions. In the workshop we presented an overview that was upbeat and positive, since we believe that the way in which distance learning is first introduced affects whether the participants will be motivated to follow through in adopting the innovation. At this awareness stage we, as change agents, wanted to present the innovation in a manner that aroused interest and curiosity.

Before conducting the faculty development workshops, we employed several strategies to generate interest in distance learning: We helped the SDMIX staff sponsor news conferences, provided press releases, and made presentations to statewide organizations and institutions. The SDMIX staff also released preworkshop publicity that included brochures, newsletters, announcements, and word-of-mouth endorsements.

We opened the workshop with a multimedia overview that delineated the goals of the workshop, highlighted each workshop segment, and introduced the SDMIX staff. This introduction was designed to set the mood for the rest of the workshop: interesting, entertaining, and informative.

PROVIDING INFORMATION ABOUT DISTANCE LEARNING

We next presented the rationale for using distance learning in South Dakota. We provided the faculty members with information that demonstrated how distance learning could meet their needs. We also discussed the time, distance, and cost barriers to the traditional delivery of continuing medical education, focusing on the high costs and negative impact on personal productivity associated with extensive travel to medical seminars.

TEACHING DISTANCE LEARNING TECHNIQUES

Teaching users appropriate instructional methods is essential to the successful adoption of a distance learning system. From reading literature reviews we knew that failure to implement an innovative program is often attributable not to the technology but to the number of process obstacles faced by the users. One such obstacle we addressed was the process of content development. We presented guidelines for identifying appropriate objectives, selecting media, and choosing instructional methods. We discussed strategies for structuring distance learning programs, increasing student interaction, and personalizing distance instruction. Much of the content was presented in a distance learning format to reduce faculty members' concern about the effectiveness of distance learning: When they saw how much they were learning, they clearly understood the effectiveness of this form of delivery. In this segment we also discussed the selection and use of support materials such as printed handouts, slides, X-ray films, overheads, and videotapes.

CHANGING PRESENTERS' ATTITUDES AND BEHAVIORS

The final strategy we employed to reduce users' concerns was to have each faculty member present the 15-minute segment he or she had designed for distance instruction. Because this segment took place after the participants had returned to their home communities, they had to access the SDMIX network from locations around the state and use their own office equipment to connect with the other participants. We encouraged them to use authentic support materials from their practices, such as X rays, slides, handouts, and videotapes.

This segment of the workshop was designed to be as realistic as possible. The faculty members followed the same protocols they would have followed if they had been presenting a statewide network program. Each participating location had a moderator who welcomed the class, conducted a roll call of all the participating locations, presented an overview of the program, and introduced each faculty member. After each faculty member presented his or her program, the moderator reviewed the key points and encouraged those at other sites to ask questions of the presenter. After each presentation, the SDMIX staff and the other faculty members provided feedback to the presenter on the quality of the program. The feedback session was kept positive and constructive to avoid discouraging the presenters from using distance learning in the future.

The results from evaluations of many such workshops indicated that we were successful in providing the faculty members with the skills and confidence they needed to use the distance learning system. Our analysis of the level of concern expressed by the participants convinced us that these workshop experiences also significantly reduced the concerns the faculty had regarding the adoption of the distance learning system.

HELPING STUDENTS ADAPT TO DISTANCE LEARNING

Most of the potential students in a distance learning system, if asked before they have tried the system, will say that they prefer traditional methods of teaching and learning. These are the methods with which they are most familiar and therefore most comfortable. Additionally, the benefits of a change from the traditional classroom format to the distance learning format may be less readily apparent to learners than they are to instructors or to the organization as a whole. As a result, many of those who will be taught or trained via a newly adopted distance learning system will initially be suspicious of the change and doubt their ability to participate effectively.

Most student reservations and concerns can be addressed through a strong system of learner support. Designing and implementing learner support mechanisms constitute an important aspect of the design and delivery of distance learning programs.

Bridging the Distance.   All learners benefit from the availability of high-quality support, and for distance learners these services are especially important. The separation between learners and instructors introduces more than a physical gap that needs to be bridged.

The psychological gap that can result from physical separation also has to be bridged, and this is accomplished largely through a strong learner support system that includes the provision of channels for interactive communication, learning resources, and communications support, all of which can enhance the distance learning experience.

Channels for Interaction.   One important form of student support is the provision of channels for interaction with the instructor and other students. When students know that physical separation does not prevent access to the instructor or their fellow learners, they feel more psychologically connected and committed to the learning project and the learning group. Effective use of both synchronous (e.g., audioconferencing) and asynchronous (e.g., computer conferencing) forms of communication and interaction can allow the formation of strong bonds between participants in a distance learning class. For example, in his research on students in three master of technology programs, William Souder found that through their interactions the students developed a sense of connection, a "kindred spirit," that was strengthened by their common experience of physical separation from the instructor and from each other.[9]

Learning Resources.   The provision of appropriate learning resources is another form of student support that takes on additional dimensions in the distance learning context. When students take courses on a university campus or in the home office of an organization, most of the learning resources they need are readily accessible in libraries and resource centers. When students are spread out in many locations, often at a significant distance from resource collections, access to the learning resources needed to complete assignments or projects becomes a serious issue. You have to make sure that the students in your distance learning courses have adequate access to supporting material, whether through instructor-identified on-line resources or at local libraries near their homes or workplaces.

Communications Support.   Whereas the need to interact with other participants and access learning resources is common to all learning environments, the need for communications support is unique to the distance learning context. In face-to-face learning situations messages are not technologically mediated; that is, they do not pass through a communications technology on their way from the originators to the receivers. In distance learning situations, however, all communication depends on technology of some sort. As a result, learners need two new kinds of support: that which orients them to the new environment and that which ensures that communications channels function smoothly and, as much as possible, transparently (that is, unobtrusively).

Frequently Asked Questions.   Through the use of techniques such as "hands-on" orientation sessions and frequently asked questions (FAQs), you can effectively counter much of the anxiety new distance learners understandably feel during their early experiences with this mode of instruction. Early and thorough orientations are well worth the time and effort spent on them, since establishing a reasonable level of learner comfort and confidence in one's ability to succeed in this new learning environment greatly increases the chances of individual and program success.

Help Desks.   Distance learners need to be supported in the use of technology. Two major issues in this area are availability and reliability. Technological support organizations such as "help desks" and customer service centers need to be available to learners at times and through channels accessible and convenient to them. For large distance learning systems, telephone call centers or Internet call centers can be established which provide 7×24 service (seven days a week, 24 hours a day). High-quality technological support can forestall delays or interruptions in communication that can detract from the effectiveness of distance learning experiences.

MONITORING AND EVALUATING SYSTEM QUALITY AND SUCCESS

As with any other organizational process and procedure, a distance learning system must undergo periodic evaluations, and evaluation is also an important part of the design of distance learning systems and programs. You will need to monitor the results of your distance learning initiatives to justify the initial investment, make decisions about continuing and/or expanding programs, and improve the processes and outcomes of the system.

The criteria for the success of a distance learning system depend largely on the context within which the system operates. In business contexts success is closely tied to a program's ability to meet the training needs of the organization within which the system operates.

These needs center on employees' efficient and cost-effective acquisition of a variety of task-oriented skills. Thus, the primary measure
of effectiveness will be a program's ability to generate improved performance in individuals and in the organization as a whole.

In an educational context success is related primarily to the
ability of the distance learning program to meet the learning needs
of the students. These needs relate to individually and socially
defined goals that can be attained in a variety of ways and represent
a broad range of learning outcomes. Although the overarching goal
is to ensure that performance standards are met, the assessment
process necessarily involves the evaluation of a number of factors
on two distinct levels of operation: the system level and the individual level.

Evaluation on the System Level

Duning, Van Kekerix, and Zaborowski[10] suggest that distance learning systems should be evaluated in three areas: the functional, the
managerial, and the instructional. The functional focus, which often
predominates in newly implemented systems, relates to technical
and/or design activities involving equipment and technical support
staff. Also included here is the appropriateness of the matchup
between delivery technologies and the requirements of instructors,
learners, and the course or training content as well as the fit between
the technical features of the system and the organization's mission
and resources.

Managerial quality and effectiveness focus on the ability to build
and maintain critical internal and external relationships. Key relationships include those with other subsystems within the organization
and those with instructors, students, and the various personnel who
facilitate and support the operation of the distance learning system.
Three criteria for managerial effectiveness are clarity, flexibility, and
consistency with the organization's mission and values.

The third area of concern—program outcomes—has traditionally
focused on factors such as completion rates and overall levels of student achievement. Duning, Van Kekerix, and Zaborowski argue that
these traditional measures are inadequate, since they neglect the
issue of congruence between organizational values and program outcomes. To overcome this limitation, they suggest that the factors of
equity, climate, autonomy, and relationship also be monitored.
Although these factors may be difficult to quantify, tracking them is

one way to encourage a focus on putting the organization's values into practice.[11]

EVALUATION ON THE INDIVIDUAL LEVEL

Perhaps the most immediate and obvious measure of program effectiveness focuses on the quality of the individual learning experience. Factors to consider in assessing effectiveness include the amount learned, the integration of learned skills into practice, and self-reported satisfaction with the learning experience. The emphasis given to each factor depends to a large extent on the learning context. In training contexts, for example, the primary emphasis is likely to be on the amount learned and the integration of new skills into the work environment. The evaluation is based on established criteria for learning and will be conducted through the use of testing techniques and structured performance measures. Learner and instructor satisfaction also can affect the amount and integration of learning and therefore should be monitored.

AMOUNT LEARNED

A primary reason for providing educational experiences or training, whether face-to-face or at a distance, is to bridge a gap that has been identified between current knowledge and a desired or necessary level of knowledge. In informal educational settings, assessment of the extent to which this gap has been closed generally is left to the individual learner. In formal education or training situations, however, structured and often standardized procedures generally are used to measure how much has been learned.

Once a learning gap has been identified, the instructors, sometimes with input from the learners, develop objectives to provide a framework within which to structure content, learning activities, and course assignments. The evaluation or assessment activities then focus on measuring the extent to which students have completed the assignments or satisfied the requirements stated in the course objectives.

As can be seen from this brief discussion, the rationale for measuring the amount learned by an individual distance learner is identical to that for assessing the learning of a traditional student or trainee. However, the strategies and procedures used in such measurement may have to be modified to fit the distance learning environment.

STRATEGIES FOR MEASURING LEARNING

The strategies used to measure what and how much has been learned depend primarily on the type of learning involved (e.g., information, attitude, or application) and the purpose of the assessment (e.g., providing feedback to the learner or judging performance). Many traditional forms of assessment, such as reports, projects, and tests, are as appropriate in a distance learning situation as they are in face-to-face instructional settings. However, because of the separation of learners and instructors, the logistics of various forms of assessment differ from traditional procedures.

Written reports, for example, have to be submitted to the instructor by mail, fax, or E-mail. Students can present individual or group projects to the instructor and to distant classmates in a variety of ways, depending on the technology used for instruction. Audioconferencing and videoconferencing allow for real-time presentation and evaluation, while in Web-based courses students can post their projects to a class bulletin board for presentation, ongoing discussion, and assessment.

Testing distance learners in skills acquisition or knowledge gains requires attention to several issues. Although skills testing may seem incompatible with distance learning, this process can be carried out in a variety of ways, depending on the skills and delivery technologies. Audioconferencing allows one to assess verbal skills such as the presentation of new product information and interviewing skills. Videoconferencing offers the addition of a video channel that may be essential for real-time assessment of and feedback about physical skills or combinations of physical and verbal skills. Although in a few situations you may need to visit the distant sites for the purpose of testing, experience has shown that you can teach and assess a wide variety of skills by using distance technology. For example, Lockheed's technical training department has successfully used videoconferencing for hands-on training and assessment of NASA personnel in "launch-critical" skills.[12]

Content testing for distance learners is in many ways similar to the testing of students in face-to-face classes. One can effectively use traditional essay, multiple-choice, or short answer tests with distance learners, although the "handing out" and "collecting" of tests must be done differently at a distance. It is possible to mail, fax, E-mail, or post tests on the Web, and students can return the tests through the same channels within the agreed-upon time frame.

Test security also can be an issue. How can instructors separated by time and/or distance from their students know for sure who has answered the questions on the test? Most classes in which groups of students come together at distant sites—audioconferencing and videoconferencing classes, for example—use on-site coordinators for course management tasks such as distributing handouts and collecting assignments. In these classes the on-site coordinator can also act as a proctor for examinations. In cases where learners form "groups of one," as in many Web-based classes, they can be required to arrange for an approved test proctor—often someone at their place of work—who follows guidelines provided by the organization that arranges the education or training.

You also may want to consider alternative ways to structure and measure the outcomes of education and training at a distance, particularly in relation to the value of traditional approaches to testing. For some learners, especially those at all levels of the formal educational system, building a knowledge base of general information and learning abstract concepts are vital parts of preparatory education. However, the learning needs of adults in work-related education and training programs are often quite different. For these learners, classes that emphasize applied rather than abstract knowledge better meet their needs and those of their organizations. This situation has important implications for the assessment of learning and particularly for the use of tests.

When learners focus on real-world problems, have opportunities to try out solutions, and are encouraged to reflect on the results of such applications, the learning that takes place is often deeper and more lasting than that which is focused on the short-term memorization of course content. However, this type of learning is often difficult to measure with traditional testing approaches. Learner performance on simulations and case studies based on actual situations that are likely to be faced in the work environment can provide a measure of what the students have learned and their potential for applying the new knowledge in their jobs. However, it is only by assessing the extent to which learners actually transfer what they were taught into practice that their final success can be measured.

Integration of New Knowledge into Practice

Increasingly, both training and formal education are expected to result in skills and knowledge that can be applied usefully to current and anticipated situations in life and professional practice. For this reason, you should try to assess the extent to which distance learning has resulted in such transference. Although in educational settings this assessment usually must be done through simulations or case studies that approximate a real-world environment, workplace settings offer opportunities for a more direct assessment of learning outcomes.

In contrast to academic settings, this kind of assessment cannot be conducted effectively by the educator but instead must be carried out by workplace supervisors through periodic performance reviews. Adequately assessing the impact of a distance learning program on employee performance requires collaboration and cooperation between instructors and workplace supervisors. When supervisors are aware of the content of training courses, they can refer specifically to the extent of transference in their performance reviews of personnel. The results of such periodic review, particularly as they relate to the distance learning program, must be fed back into the system to generate changes that will result in improved performance.

LEARNER SATISFACTION WITH DISTANCE LEARNING

We have found that learner satisfaction is an important factor in the effectiveness of a distance learning program and for that reason should be a focus of program evaluation. Satisfaction with the media and processes that make up the learning environment is a major component in a student's willingness to continue in a program or participate in further distance learning activities. In other words, a student's personal perception of the appeal of distance learning is tied to the student's level of motivation, which research has shown to be a predictor of achievement in academic settings. Although the situation may be somewhat different in business and industry, where training usually is required rather than optional, learner satisfaction still plays an important role in the successful implementation of the system.

Learner attitudes and levels of satisfaction can be assessed in several ways. Questionnaires administered partway through a course or training series can measure the level of student satisfaction with the instructional process and provide an opportunity to make a midcourse correction if the level is low. Similarly, surveys can measure end-of-course satisfaction levels. In both cases, asking learners whether they are satisfied with the distance learning experience provides a useful snapshot assessment of the current situation. Questionnaires or surveys that allow learners to note which elements in the distance learning experience contributed to or limited their satisfaction can provide more in-depth information on which to base changes in the content, structure, or process of the course or program.

Figure 7-2 provides a distance learning process evaluation survey that we have used to assess student satisfaction. The student feedback gathered from this questionnaire has helped us pinpoint areas for program and process improvements.

Interviews with individual learners or with groups of learners are another mechanism for assessing satisfaction. Although interviews are more time-consuming than questionnaires, they provide an opportunity to dialogue with learners and clarify issues.

ANALYSIS OF COST-EFFECTIVENESS

There are ways to evaluate the impact of a distance learning system in terms of savings to the organization. In Chap. 1 we explained that many companies implement distance learning systems to save money. These savings can be quantified by focusing on cost factors such as travel expenses for students, productivity costs associated with student time spent traveling, salaries and travel costs for instructional personnel, and costs for dedicated classrooms.

Many complex cost-effectiveness models have been developed by organizations to quantify their savings. A good way to structure your model is to revisit the business drivers you uncovered in the organizational needs assessment. Focus on the salient drivers and determine the factors you will use to track cost savings in the cost-efficiency analysis. Since travel cost displacement and costs associated with time lost in travel are two of the most common factors companies quantify, we recommend that you create a cost model that includes those factors. Initially, restrict the analysis to these two factors and try to hold less significant factors, such as facility leases and administrative overhead, constant in the analysis as you compare your system costs with traditional face-to-face delivery costs.

For example, assume that 1000 students will complete a three-day course at a centralized training facility. You can calculate the total annual student travel costs and salary expense associated with students' nonproductive time spent traveling. Assume that the expense for round-trip airfare and three days per diem is $1000. Eight hours of nonproductive time in travel for a student with a

NAME _____ E-MAIL ID _____

SESSION TITLE: _____ DATE: _____ LOCATION _____

DISTANCE LEARNING PROCESS EVALUATION	STRONGLY DISAGREE	DISAGREE	UNCERTAIN	AGREE	STRONGLY AGREE
Technology					
1. Student comments and questions were clear as they came over the network.					
2. The words and images on the monitors were easy to read.					
3. The technology was used effectively					
4. The course materials (media, handouts, books, etc.) were available when needed.					
Participation					
5. It was not difficult for me to pay attention.					
6. I felt comfortable asking questions and having discussions over the network.					
7. The students at my site were actively participating.					
8. I felt interaction on the network was effective.					

FIGURE 7-2. Distance learning process evaluation survey.

Presenter							
9. The presenter's voice was clear.							
10. The presenter had a voice quality that was easy to listen to.							
11. The presenter encouraged participation from students at each site.							
12. The presenter was able to tell when students had trouble understanding.							
General							
13. The on-site coordinator performed logistical tasks well.							
14. I think that distance learning is appropriate for this type of subject matter.							
15. I would participate in future distance learning courses.							
16. Overall, I felt this course was effective.							

Additional Comments:

FIGURE 7-2. (*Continued*)

$40,000 loaded salary is valued at $160 ($40,000/250 workdays per year). The total travel-related expense for the course is $1,160,000.

Note that the impact of nonproductive time on the company may be much greater if the students are sales representatives who carry a sales revenue quota of hundreds or thousands of dollars per day. They cannot meet with their customers and achieve their daily revenue objectives when they are tied up in travel.

Next, consider the cost of the distance learning equipment and support required to deliver the same course to the same 1000 students with the same instructors. For example, if the course is delivered through an Internet-based distance learning system, you need to calculate the average annual cost of any new distance learning equipment required. In this case, to reach 1000 students within a year, assume that you will need a new computer server, server software, and site licenses. Computer systems with these capabilities typically cost $100,000 annually. We will assume that students will use their existing PCs with free Internet browser software and the company LAN to access the course. We will also assume that you will require a Webmaster with a loaded salary of $60,000 to support the system and reconfigure the course content for Web-based delivery. In this example, the annual cost saving for the distance learning approach is $1 million.

If you want to construct more complex cost-efficiency models, consider including factors such as annual salary figures for all the job titles involved in the distance learning system and changes in the percentage of time each job title devotes to the project. A technology-based distance learning system typically will reduce the time commitments of the higher-paid subject matter experts and instructors. You also might want to track changes in the number of students per session, the percentage of trainees traveling, reductions in the length of individual courses, and so on. We recommend that you construct cost-efficiency models that focus on the key drivers important to the organization to keep the cost-effectiveness analysis manageable for you and comprehensible to the organization.

NOTES

1. Monson, M. 1976. *Bridging the distance,* Madison: University of Wisconsin.
2. Rogers, E. M., and F. F. Shoemaker. 1971. *Communication of innovation: A cross-cultural approach,* New York: Free Press.

3. Eraut, M. 1975. Promoting innovation in teaching and learning: Problems, processes, and institutional mechanisms. *Higher Education* 4(1): 13–26.

4. Hall, G. E. 1979. Procedures for adopting educational innovations/CBAM, using the individual and the innovation as the frame of reference for research on change. Paper presented at the annual meeting of the Australia Association for Research in Education, Melbourne, November 1979.

5. Hall, G. E., R. C. Wallace, and W. A. Dossett. 1973. A developmental conceptualization of the adoption process within educational institutions. Austin: Research and Development Center for Teacher Education, University of Texas.

6. Hancock, B. W., and A. G. Chute. 1982. Addressing the concerns of teleconference presenters through faculty development workshops. *Issues in Higher Education*, volume 6, pp. 406–407.

7. Havelock, R. G., with S. Zlotolow. 1995. *The change agent's guide*, 2d ed., Englewood Cliffs, N.J.: Educational Technology Publications.

8. Hall, 1979.

9. Souder, W. E. 1994. The effectiveness of traditional vs. satellite delivery in three management of technology master's degree programs. *American Journal of Distance Education* 7(1): 37–53.

10. Duning, B., M. Van Kekerix, and L. Zaborowski. 1993. *Reaching learners through telecommunications*, San Francisco: Jossey-Bass.

11. Duning, Van Kekerix, and Zaborowski, 1993.

12. Hosley, D. L., and S. L. Randolph. *Distance learning as a training and education tool*. Kennedy Space Center, Fla.: Lockheed Space Operations Co. ERIC Document Reproduction Service ED 355 936.

FURTHER READING

Anderson, C. W., R. R. Raszkowski, C. A. Rose, and A. G. Chute. 1983. Institutionalization of a teleconferencing network: Applying new technology in higher education. *Issues in Higher Education*, volume 9, pp. 416–422.

Bennis, W. G., K. D. Benne, R. Chin, and K. E. Corey. 1976. *The planning of change*, 3d ed., New York: Holt, Rinehart & Winston.

Chute, A. G., and L. S. Shatzer. 1996. Designing for international teletraining. *Adult Learning* (September–October): 7(1):20–21.

Chute, A. G., L. B. Balthazar, and C. O. Poston. 1990. Learning from teletraining: What the AT&T research says. In M. G. Moore (ed.). *Contemporary issues in American distance education*, Oxford, UK: Pergamon Press.

Chute, A. G., B. J. Garvin-Kester, and H. B. Bivens. 1995. *Distance learning design and delivery*, Cincinnati: AT&T.

Devlin, T. 1993. Distance training. In D. Keegan (ed.). *Theoretical principles of distance education*, New York: Routledge, 254–268.

Granger D., and T. Rocco, (eds.). 1996. *Guiding principles for distance learning in a learning society*, Washington, D.C.: American Council on Education.

Hancock, B. W., A. G. Chute, and R. R. Raszkowski. 1983. Training for teleconference instructors. In L. A. Parker and C. H. Olgren (eds.). *Teleconferencing and electronic communications,* volume 2, Madison, Wisc.: Center for Interactive Programs.

Hudspeth, D. 1997. Testing learner outcomes in Web-based instruction. In B. Kahn (ed.). *Web-based instruction,* Englewood Cliffs, N.J.: Educational Technology Publications, 353–356.

Kester, B. J., T. A. Kester, and A. G. Chute. 1995. Student response systems in corporate distance education. In E. Boschmann (ed.). *The electronic classroom,* Medford, N.J.: Learned Information Inc.

Ravitz, J. 1997. Evaluating learning networks: A special challenge for Web-based instruction. In B. Kahn (ed.). *Web-based instruction,* Englewood Cliffs, N.J.: Educational Technology Publications, 361–368.

Rogers, E. M. 1983. *Diffusion of innovations,* New York: Free Press.

Teleconferencing managers guide. 1984. Basking Ridge, N.J.: AT&T Corporation.

SYSTEM MANAGEMENT AND EXPANSION

This chapter discusses the task of managing a company's distance learning system to ensure the effective utilization of facilities and provide for reliable system performance. It also discusses the potential for expanding the scope and capabilities of a system after the infrastructure is in place and the system has been integrated into the organization's structure and processes. We end the chapter by identifying 10 areas of concern for anyone responsible for implementing and managing a distance learning system. Awareness of these problem areas can help forestall or overcome the difficulties and barriers these concerns might otherwise represent.

MANAGING A DISTANCE LEARNING SYSTEM

The management of a distance learning system is divided into two principal activities: reservations and operations. Coordination of facilities use and effective management of timelines, staffing, and promotion for a distance learning system both contribute to the success of this innovation within the organization.

RESERVATIONS

The process for reservations can be centralized, decentralized, or a mixture of the two. Setting up an efficient reservation process that fits into the overall plan is essential to the success of a distance learning program. The first decision is to choose between centralized and decentralized reservation systems. This decision depends on the number of distance learning programs that will be offered and the number of locations that will be served. Decisions also must be made regarding confirmations and cancellations, usage priorities, and dissemination of information about facilities and procedures.

Centralized or Decentralized?   In a centralized reservation system, a single person is responsible for scheduling all distance learning programs. A centralized system is highly efficient because that person knows the status of all the rooms and can negotiate with each program originator for a date and time when all the desired facilities are available. As a result, room usage throughout the system is optimized. From the user's standpoint, a centralized system makes it easy to book a distance learning course or seminar: A single call results in immediate confirmation.

In a centralized reservation system, treatment of the distance learning program's originators is uniform since only one source passes on reservation and scheduling information. Also, this type of system lends itself to the use of a telephone answering system, E-mail system, or computer database system as a means of accepting reservation requests at all hours. Some systems permit schedule lookup and on-line scheduling over the Internet.

Since a single reservation procedure serves all the locations in the system, usage stimulation and tracking are far simpler than they are when a separate set of procedures is developed for each location. An effective information program can be created for use throughout the organization, and when changes in procedures are necessary, they can be made easily by means of a single notification of the entire organization. Thus, using a centralized system eliminates a major potential source of confusion.

In a decentralized reservation system each location is responsible for scheduling its own distance learning facilities. The person at the originating location must contact the other locations to determine whether their facilities are available at the desired time. This approach offers a more "local" perspective by permitting each location to deal with its specific needs. If on-site coordinators handle the scheduling, they will be more aware of the technical capabilities and possibilities of their individual rooms.

A third type of system has worked well for some companies. With this system each location calls a centralized person to check on the availability of the other location or locations with which it wishes to conduct a distance learning program. After receiving the necessary information from the central point, the originating location proceeds to make program arrangements directly with other locations. This approach works well when the number of sites and the total number of distance learning programs is relatively small. It gives the program scheduler a quick way to find out what dates are available and an opportunity to talk to each on-site coordinator to discuss unique program requirements.

Confirmations and Cancellations.   We recommend that the person responsible for program reservations send a confirmation notice to the originator of the distance learning program and the on-site coordinators. Some electronic systems automatically send out the confirmations once the reservation is booked. This notice serves as a reminder of the date and time of the program and gives the room number and telephone number of each room involved in the program. Sending confirmation notices by mail, E-mail, or fax to all the students and on-site coordinators substantially reduces the number of phone calls needed to confirm the details of the program.

Cancellations should be handled promptly. When someone changes or cancels plans to hold a distance learning program, the program originator should notify the centralized reservation number or, in a decentralized system, the on-site coordinator in charge of the room. A statement on the confirmation form should remind the originator to advise the reservation center or on-site coordinator of cancellations promptly so that others can use the facilities. When programs are canceled less than a week before the program dates, it is a good idea to contact the on-site coordinators and students by telephone. This is especially important with video programs because there are sometimes cancellation charges when a video room or multipoint conferencing unit (MCU) is canceled less than 24 hours before the program was scheduled to start.

You need to establish clear, firm guidelines for handling usage priorities and negotiating scheduling conflicts. Since many people will want to schedule the conferencing rooms for a variety of purposes, you will have to establish priorities that can serve as guidelines when more than one group wants to use a room at the same time. One way to centralize the control of usage is to make the rooms available on a reserved basis only; this ensures that the reservation person knows the status of each room at all times. This kind of control system makes it possible to accept a reservation on very short notice with complete assurance that the room is in fact available. In developing a usage priority list, you have to decide how scheduling conflicts will be resolved and whether certain groups of users will be given priority.

We have found that the principle of first come, first served works very well in a centralized system. When two program sponsors want to use the same facility at the same time, the reservation person should try to establish a substitute program time for the second group. If this approach is not feasible, the two program organizers can be put in touch with each other to negotiate the conflict. Also, a standby list should be maintained for each time period that has been booked so that in the event of a cancellation, the group that is standing by can have the time it prefers and the facilities will not go unused because of the cancellation.

Training program reservations may be made as far in advance as one year and as close to the requested time as two weeks. This policy accommodates the desire of many training departments to create yearly projections for their programs. Also, these departments usually require a minimum of two weeks to coordinate the basic logistics for setting up a training program.

You need to decide whether local conferencing rooms may be used for other types of meetings when they are not needed for distance learning. This decision can be made by the centralized management team for all the locations or left to the managers at the individual locations, allowing each location to find the best solution for its local space problems. If local meetings are permitted in the distance learning rooms, you will have to develop guidelines for "bumping" them if the need arises. It is important to communicate these priorities clearly and act on them consistently. If all users are treated fairly, they will cooperate fully and work for the continuing success of the program.

A reservation form facilitates the process and provides valuable information. Certain items of information should be collected for each distance learning program and clearly indicated on the form the reservation person fills out. This form serves as a memory aid for the regular reservation person and guides the novice or temporary substitute through the procedure. It also provides a method of collecting information needed for tracking system use and operation.

The information you collect may vary, depending on the organization's needs. We suggest that the reservation person record the date and time of each program, being sure to specify Eastern time, Eastern

Daylight time, Central time, and so on, after each time listed. The distance learning program should be assigned a unique program number for easy reference; include the name, address, telephone number, fax number, and E-mail address of the instructors and the site each instructor will use. List the name, address, telephone number, fax number, and E-mail address of each on-site coordinator and the location he or she is handling. For each site, list the audio, video, and fax numbers in the room. Finally, include the name, address, telephone number, fax number, and E-mail address of the person requesting the booking. In addition to this basic information about the program, this form can be used to record whether a confirmation notice was sent, whether special equipment will be needed, and other types of information, such as billing numbers, if appropriate.

The reservation forms should be kept current in an electronic database that is backed up periodically. It is also a good idea to print a weekly schedule of all the programs in the system. Some network operations centers keep all program schedules in a loose-leaf binder for quick reference.

The reservation center provides a variety of services: It receives and processes requests for reservations, confirms reservations, and quotes estimates for network usage charges and provides usage information after a call has been completed. Reservation personnel also can be helpful in distributing information such as material about techniques or conferencing room capabilities.

OPERATIONS

Systems operations are the second critical aspect of system management. It is important to develop a systematic approach to the operational aspects of the distance learning network to ensure that programs are set up efficiently, the equipment is properly maintained, and each location in one's area of responsibility has a trained on-site coordinator. These operational considerations are important for establishing smooth-running, uninterrupted service and stimulating participation in distance learning programs in the organization.

Session Setup.   How you set up a distance learning session—that is, how you establish the electronic connections for the class—depends largely on staffing constraints, the amount and complexity of equipment involved, the number of locations participating, and the type of program. In a distance learning program that involves two locations, one location simply calls the other to establish the connection. This is a relatively easy procedure, and the instructor can make the connection without assistance.

To set up an audio, audiographic, or video conference involving three or more locations, some form of bridge or MCU is required. The various bridging alternatives should be discussed with the MIS or telecommunications representative. Distance learning programs generally are set up by a conference operator or are set up for the "meet-me" mode. If conference operator services are used, the operator calls the telephone or video numbers given for the remote locations at the scheduled time. If a multipoint conference is set up for the meet-me mode, each on-site coordinator is required to dial the conference bridge or MCU before the start of the program. We recommend that on-site coordinators call in at least 15 minutes before the program to make sure they have a good connection.

Internet distance learning programs do not need an on-site coordinator. The students are responsible for opening their own personal computer (PC) browsers, accessing the network, and entering the uniform resource locator (URL) (Web location) for the program.

Certain provisions should be made to ensure that the distance learning equipment is operating satisfactorily. It is common to require on-site coordinators and/or students to complete brief questionnaires at the end of each session to report any equipment problems they have encountered. These questionnaires are then submitted to the appropriate maintenance person for immediate corrective action. Generally, the local maintenance person or the on-site coordinator can deal with minor equipment problems. To forestall as many problems as possible, one should perform preventive maintenance checks the day before a scheduled program to identify problems that exist before use by the students.

In our experience, many reported problems result from operator error or improper equipment setup. The on-site coordinator should be able to recognize quickly those equipment malfunctions which require technical repair and those which do not. Many times the problem is a simple one; for example, a power cord may have become loose or students may have operated the equipment incorrectly. Such problems can be resolved quickly, and a program in progress can resume with almost no interruption. If the problem is serious, the maintenance person will prepare a trouble ticket for the manufacturer to service the equipment.

On-Site Coordinator.   The on-site coordinator can perform many valuable functions. The success of a distance learning program depends largely on the role of the on-site coordinator. Below we provide a detailed look at the logistic and administrative issues in a distance learning environment that benefit from the special attention of an on-site coordinator.

An on-site coordinator (also called a remote coordinator or a teleconference room manager) is an important member of the distance learning team. Since many students will be new to distance learning, their familiarity with the procedures and equipment may be minimal or nonexistent. The presence of an on-site coordinator helps eliminate some of the factors that lead to stress for both the instructor and the students who are new to the environment. The presence of the on-site coordinator takes some of the emphasis off the technology, allowing students to focus more on the program content than on the delivery medium. The human touch provided by a knowledgeable and enthusiastic on-site coordinator can be a welcome and comforting element in a new environment and can contribute greatly to the success of a distance learning program.

The on-site coordinator can give open demonstrations as an effective way to teach new students how the equipment operates and a means of expanding the base of potential participants. The coordinator also can answer questions about equipment capabilities. Some questions may involve hands-on experimentation with the conferencing equipment, and the answers may lead to new, creative uses of distance learning approaches.

In more sophisticated and complex high-use installations, you may want to designate and train a dedicated on-site coordinator to be responsible for setting up, giving brief equipment demonstrations before each program, doing periodic checks of the equipment, and responding to any problems or questions that arise before, during, or after a program. Permanently locating the on-site coordinator near the distance learning and teleconferencing rooms will contribute to the security of the rooms and equipment.

Following are some of the ways in which an on-site coordinator can contribute to the success of the overall distance learning program:

- Promote a positive attitude toward videoconferencing
- Set up and test all the equipment
- Set up the communication links for the program
- Greet the students as they arrive
- Explain and demonstrate the use of the equipment

- Assure that various student materials are distributed when required
- Be available in case of a problem
- Provide emergency backup or contact information
- Administer evaluations if required by the instructor
- Monitor off-line group discussions and casework if required
- Serve as a spokesperson and a liaison between remote students and the instructor when appropriate
- Return materials (audio, visual, evaluations, etc.) to the instructor at the end of the session

Since the on-site coordinator is normally not in the distance learning room for the entire program, some of the logistic responsibilities can be shared by the students. Throughout the course these responsibilities should be rotated among the students so that no single student feels overburdened by chores that detract from his or her primary responsibility: to learn.

Distance Learning Program Timeline. The administration of a distance learning program is more complex than that of a face-to-face program since two or more locations are involved. Sufficient time must be built into the planning process to allow for scheduling sites, shipping materials, and testing equipment with the remote sites. You may have to rely on on-site coordinators to manage parts of the logistics before and after as well as during the program. Keep in mind that you will not be on the spot at each site to handle problems if they occur. The more up-front planning and preparation you do, the more confidence you will have that the program will run smoothly.

The timeline for planning and managing all the activities for a distance learning program vary across different training organizations. As you create a timeline for your distance learning programs, try to keep the steps and intervals in line with current practice for the organization's traditional training programs. After years of experience with distance learning programs, we recommend the following step-by-step implementation timeline for each program offered. This timeline is based on the assumption that you have already ordered and installed the required equipment at each site and have trained the people on the distance learning "team" (see below for a discussion of the composition of this team). If you are installing new equipment at any of the sites, make sure the installation is complete before the corresponding dates on the timeline. The suggested timeline allows ample time to address all the required steps for each distance learning program.

Job Aid: Distance Learning Program Timeline

Activity	Person Responsible	Time before Program	Due Date
1. Identify the program(s) to be delivered.	_____	3–4 months	_____
2. Determine the locations involved (based on student demand).	_____	3–4 months	_____
3. Identify on-site coordinator(s).	_____	3–4 months	_____
4. Select program dates.	_____	3–4 months	_____
5. Reserve rooms, bridge, or MCU and any equipment required (e.g., videotape players).	_____	3–4 months	_____
6. Notify potential students of program availability.	_____	2–3 months	_____
7. Obtain instructor assistant and/or subject matter expert commitment (if applicable).	_____	2–3 months	_____
8. Prepare slides, handouts, computer graphics, videotapes and preprogram material.	_____	1–2 months	_____
9. Prepare a short biography of instructor.	_____	1–2 months	_____
10. Write the student welcome letter if appropriate.	_____	1 month	_____
11. For smaller programs, obtain names, addresses, and telephone numbers of all the students. Call students in advance to welcome them.	_____	3 weeks	_____
12. For smaller programs, prepare master roster.	_____	3 weeks	_____
13. Distribute welcome letter, preprogram materials, background and biographical sheet, and master roster to students.	_____	2 weeks	_____
14. Distribute materials to on-site coordinator(s) (evaluation forms, handouts, student list, all bridge numbers).	_____	2 weeks	_____
15. Contact on-site coordinator(s) to ensure receipt of all materials.	_____	1 week	_____
16. Conduct a dry run of the program with on-site coordinator(s). (Use this time to review program plan and answer any questions.)	_____	1 week	_____

Day of Delivery

1. Connect all sites to bridge of MCU.	_____	15 minutes	_____
2. Conduct the program.	_____	_____	_____
3. Return extra materials and evaluations to trainer.	_____	ASAP	_____

Staffing Considerations. The total number of professional and technical staff members required to operate a distance learning system depends on a number of considerations. The overall size of the distance learning system in terms of the number of sites and the number of students served annually is the major determinant of staff size. In small training departments the distance learning staff unit may consist of a part-time manager who has to do the planning, programming, and operations. Large corporatewide systems can require 10 to 40 people to staff an entire district. It is common to find distance learning systems that employ a combination of dedicated resource personnel and part-time project personnel who report to the distance learning general manager in a matrix reporting relationship.

A typical midsize distance learning system will have personnel assigned to four functional areas: planning, administration, operations, and programming. The number of people in each functional area depends on the number of programs offered, students served, and sites on the network. Even the largest systems started small and grew as training demands and the number of students increased.

The distance learning general manager will be responsible for budgeting, staffing, strategic planning, and overall unit performance. An administrative manager will be responsible for scheduling, reservations, revenue and expense tracking, and general office management. An operations manager will have the responsibility for technical operations, system troubleshooting, and procurement of equipment for system expansion. A programming manager, often called a performance technologist, will have oversight responsibility for the design, development, and marketing of the educational programs offered in the distance learning system.

Often instructors are not part of the distance learning system group; instead, they report to a curriculum delivery group such as the sales training unit. Similarly, the on-site coordinator generally reports to the branch office managers at the remote sites. Evaluation services often are outsourced to ensure an objective interpretation of student questionnaires and interview data. In some cases university faculty members or graduate interns are employed to assist with evaluation projects.

Clerical personnel generally are assigned to the four functional groups and have the responsibility for the day-to-day support operations of the distance learning system. Their duties include routine communication with the on-site coordinators, registering students, making reservations for the audio bridge or MCU, testing the connection to the remote sites, mailing or faxing program materials to the remote locations, compiling students' test data, and maintaining network utilization reports.

The following guidelines describe the number and types of support personnel that may be needed for a distance learning system, although your actual needs will depend on the factors discussed above. We suggest the following matchups of organizational needs and resource personnel to ensure the effectiveness of the distance learning network.

- An audio network that reaches an average of 50,000 internal students a year with one-hour weekly information update programs employs one general manager, one administrative manager, one operations manager, and two clerical support persons. Instructor resources come from the headquarters marketing organization.

- An audiographic network that reaches 3000 external client students a year with courses that average one day in length employs a general manager, an administrative manager, an operations manager, a program manager, and two clerical persons. Instructor and developer resources are part of the organization's client education curriculum group.

- A video network that reaches 2000 internal students a year with courses that average two days in length employs a general manager, an administrative manager, an operations manager, a part-time senior performance technologist, and two clerical persons. Instructor and developer resources are part of a management curriculum unit.

- A Web-based information resource unit that receives over 150,000 hits on its Web site each year and responds to 1000 E-mail and telephone requests a year employs one full-time Webmaster and two part-time Web programmers. Other units develop the actual informational content hosted on the Web-site, and the MIS organization provides the Web server. Once the Web site information has been hosted on the Web site, the total number of staff support hours needed decreases dramatically; a Web system automatically handles student access requests and the delivery of content without direct staff support.

A good way to determine appropriate staffing guidelines for a distance learning system is to refer to the staffing requirements for related training units within the organization and benchmark the competition to determine how it has handled similar project requirements.

Promoting a Distance Learning System.   We have touched on the subject of promotion in terms of building support for distance learning as a part of organizational change. We review some of those ideas here from the perspective of promotion as an ongoing function that is necessary both in the early stages of implementation and for a fully implemented, completely integrated distance learning system.

Organizational change does not stop after an innovation has been implemented; ongoing promotional efforts have to be modified periodically to reflect changes both in the organization as a whole and in the distance learning system. Continued promotion will ensure that people at all levels of the organization are kept up to date on the activities and benefits of *their* distance learning system. Just as your direction helped guide the choices of systems, equipment, and room design, your guidance as an internal marketing manager is needed to ensure that the system is used to its full potential. Effective promotion will help you develop the broad base of support and use needed for system maintenance and expansion.

Developing a Committed User Base.   The first step is to identify and expand a committed user base. You want to make sure that everyone in the company who can benefit from the distance learning system is made aware of its existence, educated in its use, and encouraged or motivated to use it. Every successful and satisfied distance learner helps spread the word, and good word of mouth is the best kind of advertising. Additionally, continuously adding to the user base will increase the cost-efficiency of distance education or training, one of an organization's main objectives in implementing such a system.

Developing a committed user base may be difficult at first. You probably developed an appreciation of the value of distance learning while working through the needs assessment, planning, and implementation phases of the project. It would be a mistake, however, to assume that your knowledge of and enthusiasm for distance learning are shared by all the intended users. Quite the opposite may be true for a variety of reasons.

As we have seen, both potential instructors and potential students often share anxieties related to this innovation. Unfamiliarity with this mode of teaching and learning is of course a common reason for hesitancy about using distance learning. Another often overlooked misgiving is the concern of some instructors and students that distance learning will eliminate their travel altogether: Travel is viewed by many people as a "perk" of the job that they are reluctant to give up.

Instructors may be concerned about difficulty in using equipment, loss of the social contact that normally is associated with training programs, and the need to learn new skills. They will be willing to adopt the system only after they perceive it as an improvement over the present means of communication and instruction.

However, some of the company's potential instructors and students may be open and receptive to the idea of substituting distance learning for many face-to-face training programs: They may be "burned out" on travel or eager to learn how to use the new communications technologies they have heard so much about. This group will expect to be informed about this new capability, told how to use it, and convinced that it will help them do their jobs better.

Promotional Techniques.   Your goal in promoting the concept of distance learning to potential users is to move them through the adoption process to the establishment of a base of repeat users. Techniques such as publicity in internal publications, newsletters, posters, and executive endorsements can be effective ways to gain user attention and stimulate interest in distance learning and its benefits. You can schedule seminars and training sessions and then use your personal persuasion skills to get potential users to participate in these live demonstrations of distance learning. You also can schedule promotional programs on an ongoing basis to provide continuing reminders of the benefits of distance learning and generate renewed interest through a changing series of relevant applications.

In all your promotional activities you should carefully avoid making exaggerated and unsupportable claims about the benefits of the organization's distance learning system. Instead, you should seek to convey genuine enthusiasm for the many benefits of the system by means of evaluative reports and endorsements by satisfied users.

Top-Level Support.   Getting key executives to endorse and use the system is important to the success of any distance learning system. The advocacy of a key person or small group of people high in the organization is the most persuasive kind of endorsement. When other potential users know that key executives solidly endorse and use the new system, your efforts to promote usage will pay off more quickly.

This show of support may take several forms. Schedule seminars for VIPs and make a presentation that describes the physical setup of the system, lists the benefits in terms of costs and productivity, and demonstrates how the system works. Ask key upper-level executives to send memos to division or department heads and potential users to communicate the objectives of the distance learning program and explain how it helps advance the overall goals of the organization. Place articles in company publications featuring interviews with executives on the subject of distance learning.

Targeting Unit Needs.   We explained earlier the importance of targeting needs that have been identified by the different units in the organization. In planning the internal promotion program, you should first review what you know about the targeted units and then go back to all those units and make certain they understand that the organization has designed and implemented a distance learning system that can meet their needs. As you prepare the promotional materials, make sure the specific needs and benefits to these user groups are emphasized.

The central message of all promotional material should be the benefits of distance learning. Your approach should be both specific and personal. Emphasize how distance learning meets individual needs and identify rewards for using the system. When potential users understand the benefits to themselves, see how easily they can learn to use the system, and have experienced it successfully, they will spread the word and help expand the user base.

Addressing Unspoken User Concerns.   Overcoming unspoken fears about using new technology, especially sophisticated distance learning systems, is part of this effort. Make sure students know what to expect, ensure them of your willingness to answer questions, and be ready to deliver ongoing support for all the users of the distance learning system.

Many unspoken questions focus on potential users' fear that they will be unable to master the technology. Another unspoken question in the minds of every potential user is, What's in it for me? In the promotional materials stress that distance learning can help instructors and students save time by avoiding extensive travel and the discomforts associated with it. Many instructors will see a personal benefit when they discover that they can increase their influence within the company by helping more students develop professionally: Distance learning empowers them to be in more than one place at a time. To others, the idea of being on the leading edge of a new innovation is a motivating benefit.

Establishing Ongoing Promotion.   A strong reminder campaign can help keep distance learning in the forefront of potential users' awareness. By continuing to stress a variety of benefits, features, and new applications, you can keep the channels of communication open to these current nonusers. As a result, they will be ready to give distance learning a try when they encounter a suitable application.

The longer the system is in use, the more "fans" it will develop and the more success stories those satisfied users will generate. Make it a point to take advantage of this growing body of enthusiastic learners by encouraging them to become advocates for distance learning. Publish "I did it!" articles in the organization's publications and invite experienced users to become cotrainers in beginner group training sessions.

Experienced instructors also should be involved in promoting the distance learning system. You may wish to establish user groups or special interest groups in which instructors can provide inspiration, information, and support. The instructors can help promote system use and acceptance by presenting testimonials and suggesting new applications to potential instructors.

SYSTEM EXPANSION

Once the technological infrastructure is in place and operating smoothly, you may want to seek out other potential users to share the benefits of the distance learning system as well as the costs of sustaining and expanding it. It is unlikely, especially in the initial stages of implementation, that any single training unit will use the system infrastructure to its full capacity. Partnerships with other training units can ensure that the system receives maximum use and that its benefits are shared throughout the organization.

EXPANDING USE ACROSS DEPARTMENTS

While many distance learning systems are implemented to meet a specific need in one division or department in an organization, use of the system can spread quickly to related departments. For example, an update program series that works well for the sales department probably will have applications in the marketing department. Human resources programs such as diversity training, benefits updates, retirement planning seminars, and safety briefings will have horizontal application in various organizational departments. In fact, a distance learning system will encourage training managers to begin to identify opportunities for sharing other training programs across the company.

EXPANDING PROGRAM CATEGORIES

After users experience one type of distance learning program, they will be disposed to experiment with other types or categories of these programs. A training organization usually starts by offering distance learning courses that replace those which formerly were delivered face to face in the training facility. They then move toward distance delivery of some of the shorter update programs that supplement the normal programs.

Look first for educational and training program categories that are commonplace in the organization today and then consider program categories and training formats that are not being used, perhaps because of cost or lack of human resources. This process probably will suggest a number of educational and training program categories that are good candidates for a distance learning program. We have found distance delivery to be appropriate for the following program categories:

- Formal classroom instruction.
- Regularly scheduled update programs.
- Special or nonrecurring programs such as those focused on policy changes or new and/or revised procedures.
- One-way broadcast presentations to large audiences. These presentations may be synchronous satellite video broadcasts or asynchronous programs hosted on the Web that students can access seven days a week, 24 hours a day.
- Multisite orientation programs for new hires that feature key executives "brought in" by distance learning technology.

Initially, try distance delivery of one program type or category. When this has been successful, you will feel more comfortable extending distance learning program offerings to other categories.

MEETING INDUSTRY SEGMENT TRAINING REQUIREMENTS

Any consideration of adding new distance learning applications must focus on the ways in which training interventions can meet employee and organizational needs. Below we describe some of the most common training needs for various industry segments and the specific benefits distance learning offers in those contexts.

Financial Services

- Continuing education for graduate degrees, advanced certification, and so on
- In-company education about new strategic directions, desktop financial tools, and changes in tax laws
- Training to ensure that employees' financial planning skills are competitive within the industry
- Bringing new investment products and analysis tools quickly on line

Health Care

- Continuing medical education
- Grand rounds and specialty council seminars
- Training of medical students and residents
- Patient education programs

Retail

- In-store employee training in basic skills
- Required safety programs
- Multisite new employee orientation sessions with company executives
- New products and new sales updates

Insurance

- Continuing education for graduate degrees (MBAs)
- Professional development, including Certified Life Underwriter (CLU) certification
- Training in strategic directions and new products for regional office employees
- New analysis and actuarial tools quickly and effectively brought on-line by knowledgeable users

Government

- Courses by subject matter experts on operations across the city, state, or country
- Training of military personnel for civilian jobs under defense conversion initiatives
- Education in new aspects of computer programs

PROGRAM EXAMPLES

Among the thousands of distance learning programs that have been implemented successfully, most share common characteristics. Distance learning systems connect geographically dispersed employees with distributed learning resources. They save time and travel costs as they bring required continuing education programs to students. Following is a selection of brief case examples representing various types of successful distance learning programs.

- The sales department of a pharmaceutical company used audioconferencing to reach new audiences. The department brought together groups of physicians and nurses for continuing education seminars to discuss new treatments for psychological disorders. In one case groups of health care professionals gathered at over 200 hospitals across the country to review medical case histories with national experts.
- The research and development (R&D) department of a corporation had its management staff at one location and its operations staff at another location. It dispensed with travel to a centralized training location and instead used combinations of audio and video distance learning technologies to conduct periodic training seminars on new product introductions.
- A human resources (HR) department delivered video distance learning seminars to bring managers and employees up to date on recent government regulations affecting their HR policies. The programs included equal employment opportunity (EEO) reviews and training involving the implications of new legislation.
- An automobile corporation used a nationwide distance learning satellite broadcast to introduce a new line of car models and describe sales incentives to its sales staff and dealers.

- Using two-way interactive video, professors at a major university addressed three classrooms full of students at corporate sites to explain the impact of the new telecommunications act. The two-day program used a combination of lectures followed by question-and-answer periods.

- Engineers in an aircraft manufacturing company used video tele-conferencing to train commercial aircraft pilots nationwide on how to evaluate perceptions of new aircraft in test situations and at the same time study visual representations of the systems involved.

- A consortium of universities offered a distinguished lecturer series via video-based distance learning to national and international locations. A key benefit of the system was that far more students had access to the faculty experts than could have attended a conventional class.

- A government agency used video distance learning technology to reduce the amount of time required to train field personnel. All the employees at remote locations were able to receive the same information at the same time, and groups at all sites benefited from the presence of subject matter experts.

- To deliver professional engineering education, a video distance learning network established hundreds of "satellite" instructional centers across the country. The system offered advanced professional degrees and continuing education credits.

- The new-business development unit of a corporation uses Internet-based distance learning to introduce new concepts. The concepts are presented in tutorials, and students are encouraged to engage in the idea sharing and chat capabilities of the on-line system.

- A corporation uses an Internet-based knowledge "warehouse" to train its sales staff on product features and benefits. It also delivers product change announcements to the entire sales organization to educate its members about major changes in the company's products or services, especially when the products and services have important legal or competitive implications.

Broad ranges of training categories make up the mix of training deliverables today. The decentralized, regionalized nature of many organizations brings with it a number of problems associated with the ongoing process of continuing professional education, development, and training. Considerable distances can separate employees in different functions and even those within the same function.

Audio, audiographic, video, and Internet distance learning can bridge those distances.

WATCH YOUR STEP! TEN COMMON MISTAKES THAT CAN SABOTAGE A DISTANCE LEARNING SYSTEM

Chapters 5 through 8 addressed implementation factors critical to the success of a distance learning system. Over the past 25 years we have observed hundreds of distance learning systems, some of them very successful and others not so successful. Below we list 10 common mistakes that can sabotage efforts to implement a distance learning system in an organization.

1. *There is no clear statement of need for the system.*   The support staff, instructors, and administrators must understand the compelling individual and organizational needs driving the establishment of the distance learning system. You need to be ready with a clear and concise answer to the question, Why are we doing this? The distance learning staff must be able to articulate both the needs and the ways in which the distance learning system will address them.

2. *There is no visible champion for the distance learning system.* There must be at least one person in a leadership position within the organization who is a visible champion for the distance learning initiative. This person must have passion for the project and the perseverance to stay the course when challenges surface. The champion also must be able to inspire others to support and participate in the initiative.

3. *There is no organizational commitment to change.*   An organizational commitment to create and sustain the distance learning initiative is imperative, and this commitment must be tangible as well as ideological. Adequate staff and financial support signals real organizational commitment and facilitates the integration of the initiative into the culture and structure of the organization.

4. *A marketing plan does not exist.*   Merely having a better alternative to traditional training delivery is not enough. You need to develop a marketing plan to keep the staff and users focused on the vision, mission, and benefits of the distance learning initia-

tive. The marketing plan should specify how you intend to promote distance learning internally to the support staff and externally to potential students.

5. *Cross-functional teaming is absent.* The success of a distance learning system requires cross-functional teaming among stakeholders from the training department, telecommunications department, MIS department, and end users' units. Those who have a stake in the success of the system need to jointly identify and address any concerns or issues relating to the training process or technology requirements before delivering the first program. A mechanism for tracking and resolving cross-functional issues is helpful.

6. *Programs are not designed for the distance learning context.* The training department must recognize that the design of materials for distance learning should differ from the design of materials for traditional training programs. The elements of the distance learning program—learning objectives, instructional methods, interaction techniques, content, delivery technologies, and the evaluation plan—must all complement each other.

7. *There are insufficient support services for distance learners.* The organization needs to provide learner support services comparable to or better than those taken for granted in a traditional training environment. The support services should include access to library information services, advising, registration, counseling, technical help desks, and on-site coordinator support.

8. *The intended learning outcomes are inappropriate for the medium.* The stakeholders may have unrealistic expectations about the outcomes of distance learning programs. Programs should be organized around demonstrable learning outcomes, help the students achieve those outcomes, and assess students' progress by reference to those outcomes.

9. *The technology infrastructure is inadequate.* The organization's technology infrastructure plan has to support the distance learning system's goals and activities. The technology infrastructure selected has to be reliable and have the power necessary to support its intended use. The goal for technology use is that it become "transparent"; that is, the equipment should not distract students from the learning tasks, and the students should find the equipment accessible and relatively easy to operate.

10. *There is no reward and recognition program.* People undergo-

ing a change process often ask, What's in it for me? Change is difficult for most people, and they need to feel that their effort to break away from things that are familiar and embrace something new is personally worthwhile. The champion and the organization have to identify tangible ways to recognize and reward people who contribute to the establishment of the new distance learning system.

We know that distance learning works and can bring enormous benefits to organizations. We also know that implementing successful distance learning initiatives can be a source of great personal satisfaction to those responsible. However, some distance learning initiatives seem to get bogged down during the planning or implementation stage and never reach their potential for usefulness. Being aware of some of the common barriers to successful implementation can help you avoid problems and increase the chance that your efforts to bring distance learning to the organization will be successful.

FURTHER READING

Chute, A. G. 1990. Strategies for implementing teletraining systems. *Educational and Training Technology International* 27(3): 264–270.

Chute, A. G., and J. L. Elfrank. 1990. Teletraining: Needs, solutions and benefits. *International Teleconferencing Association Yearbook 1990,* Washington, D.C.: ITCA.

Chute, A. G., M. K. Hulick, C. Messmer, and B. W. Hancock. 1986. Teletraining in the corporate environment. In L. A. Parker and C. H. Olgren (eds.). *Teleconferencing and electronic media,* volume 4, Madison, Wisc.: Center for Interactive Programs.

Teleconferencing managers guide. 1984. Basking Ridge, N.J.: AT&T Corporation.

SPECIAL ISSUES FOR EDUCATIONAL INSTITUTIONS

The focus of most of our discussions so far has been on using distance learning to meet training needs in the corporate sector. Much of what we have presented applies equally well in educational settings: Distance learning can provide solutions for educational as well as business organizations. However, the fact that education and training differ in several significant ways between educational and business organizations makes it important to address issues that relate specifically to distance learning in educational institutions.

DIFFERENCES BETWEEN EDUCATION AND TRAINING

SCOPE AND FOCUS

Most definitions of the term *education*, such as that developed by the United Nations Educational, Scientific, and Cultural Organization (UNESCO), describe it as a general rather than specific activity: "organized and sustained instruction designed to communicate a combination of knowledge, skills, and understanding valuable for all the activities of life."[1] Also common to many views of education is the idea of developing both a depth and a breadth of knowledge and understanding. Especially in the case of adult students, education is generally a voluntary activity in pursuit of personally identified and personally meaningful goals.

These characteristics contrast with those of training, which often focuses on the development of narrow competencies or skills that will be applied to a particular task or in a particular context. (In some cases this distinction is becoming blurred, however, as organizations increasingly provide training in more general coping and problem-solving skills in recognition of the need for employees to adjust to the rapid changes that now characterize the workplace.) Generally, decisions related to training—who will participate, what will be taught, and so forth—are made by the organization rather than by the individuals receiving the training. Similarly, the goals toward which training points are usually organizational goals (e.g., increased performance and efficiency) rather than personal goals of the trainees. These distinctions between education and training also apply to distance education versus distance training.

SETTING

The institutional settings in which distance education and distance training occur impose other differences. For example, distance training is seldom viewed as the primary product of the organizations in which it occurs. Instead, it is viewed as a support activity in organizations whose primary focus is elsewhere. Most distance education, by contrast, is the product of institutions whose primary focus is education: schools, colleges, universities, and so on. When education is the primary product of an institution, the organization establishes policies to regulate its development, implementation, and review.

INSTITUTIONAL POLICY ISSUES

The success of a distance education program that is part of a traditional campus-based institution depends on the extent to which the institution views the program as an integral part of its activities. In the past distance education programs (usually represented by correspondence units) were often viewed as marginal to the mission of the institution, and policies were more often designed to contain (or "police") the program than to support it. Increasingly, however, traditional institutions are realizing the potential of distance education to help them fulfill their institutional mission both by reaching new audiences and by serving current audiences in new and flexible ways. Increasing acceptance and support of distance education have resulted in policy development that recognizes the need to incorporate distance education programs, students, and faculty into the mainstream of the institution. Below we discuss three of the more important policy issues that have to be addressed as institutions attempt to institutionally integrate distance and resident instruction.

Residency.   Although residency requirements usually are not an issue in undergraduate programs, graduate degree programs have traditionally included an on-campus residence component so that the institution can socialize students into the field of study, provide them with access to a variety of formal and informal learning experiences, and benefit from the experience and knowledge a diverse student body brings to the university. As increasingly powerful communications technologies allow innovative approaches to graduate instruction, institutions are beginning to examine their traditional residency requirements. They are developing policies to ensure that the objectives of residency are met without putting undue restrictions on the development and implementation of new approaches to program structure and delivery. Often these policies include guidelines that suggest ways in which distance education programs can meet the objectives of specific elements of residency by using instructional technology.

For example, a common element of the residency experience is access to information and instructional resources such as libraries, laboratories, and research facilities. The objective of this element is to offer students educational experiences beyond what individual instructors can provide. In distance education programs this objective can be met in a variety of ways. Video teleconferencing, audio-conferencing, and computer conferencing all offer means to connect students directly to extrainstitutional content experts. On-line seminars and workshops with experts around the world—structured and facilitated by the instructor—greatly expand the geographic range from which these experts can be drawn. CD-ROMs, on-line searches, and electronic connections to libraries and other data collections offer access to vast collections of data and information. Course home pages can offer course-specific resources or direct students to related sources of information. Students can combine these resources with others available on site and with course content to enhance learning and expand their knowledge base.

Other residency objectives, such as out-of-class interaction between faculty members and students and among students, exposure to and socialization in the field of study, ready access to academic advising and support services, and identification with the institution, can all be met through the creative use of distance learning technologies. Institutional policies that reflect awareness and acceptance of this capability serve the interests of both the students and the institution.

Student Support Services.   Instruction is only one aspect of the educational experience. Students also need convenient access to services that provide the guidance and personal support required to complete their programs successfully and in a timely manner. Whereas on-campus students can readily access such support, institutions need to ensure that students in distance education programs receive standard support services that are comparable in scope and quality to those provided to on-campus students. Convenient and flexible access to procedures and resources such as registration, counseling, and library services is necessary to effectively integrate off-campus students into the academic community.

Students in distance education programs also need support services that focus on the technical aspects of distance learning. Institutions need to provide consistent and convenient support for whatever technological platform is used to deliver and receive instruction. This support may include advice about hardware and software purchases, assistance with technical problems, and the like.

Finally, institutions need to develop policies that establish the structure and placement of student support services: as a separate unit serving distant students, through off-campus support centers or on-line access, or as a function of the same office that serves on-campus students.

Faculty Support and Compensation.   Faculty support is another important policy issue. Teaching in a distance learning environment is often exciting and rewarding, but it can be demanding as well. Developing lessons that use the power and flexibility of modern communications technologies to bridge the distance between instructor and learners demands both new skills and innovative applications of old skills. It also requires considerably more time than does designing traditional classroom instruction. For these reasons, it is critically important to develop policies that ensure that faculty members are supported with both technical resources and institutional rewards.

Policies that commit the institution to provide faculty support such as orientation to delivery technologies, ongoing technical support, consultation with instructional designers, and teaching assistants and/or on-site coordinators take into account the fact that an institution's most important investment in a distance education program is probably the instructors who deliver the courses. Equally important is the establishment of professional reward systems that encourage faculty members to become and continue to be committed stakeholders. Policies that recognize distance teaching as "on load" rather than "overload" assignments encourage faculty members to participate and signal their support for distance education programs as valuable components of the institution's overall activities. Similarly, promotion and tenure policies that reward distance teaching on a par with classroom teaching strengthen the credibility of distance teaching both among a faculty member's peers and within the institution as a whole.

NOTES

1. Tight, M. 1996. *Key concepts in adult education and training,* New York: Routledge.

FURTHER READING

Devlin, T. 1993. Distance training. In D. Keegan (ed.). *Theoretical principles of distance education,* New York: Routledge, 254–268.

Moore, M., and M. Thompson. 1997. *The effects of distance learning,* rev. ed. ACSDE Research Monograph 15. University Park: American Center for the Study of Distance Education, Pennsylvania State University.

LOOKING AT THE PRESENT, LOOKING TO THE FUTURE

DAYS OF FUTURE PAST

Throughout this book we have focused on the methods and technologies currently used to deliver education and training at a distance. It is fascinating to consider that most of these approaches would have seemed "futuristic" in the very recent past. Many people can remember reading about or seeing videoconferencing units, communication satellites, and global computer networks as fanciful elements in science fiction novels or movies, yet today these technologies are real tools for expanding the teaching and learning repertoires of those involved in education and training.

This chapter briefly reviews some of the main points discussed in earlier chapters and then offers some futuristic speculation on developments in distance learning as the present becomes the future.

In the Introduction we looked at how changes in the workplace and in society in general are producing pressures that challenge traditional approaches to education and training. We discussed how business and industry need distance learning to help them provide high-quality training in the face of shrinking budgets, scarce resources, and a changing workforce. We also suggested that formal educational systems can benefit from distance learning approaches that can extend access to new learner populations, enhance and/or

201

expand the range of available teaching and learning "tools," and in many cases deliver education more cost-effectively. Finally, we listed 10 benefits often reported by organizations that have implemented distance learning systems and provided a number of brief examples of successful distance learning applications.

Chapter 1 focused on evidence of both the need for and benefits of distance learning solutions for many current educational and training needs. Building on the idea that knowledge needs are changing and organizational structures and cultures are changing in response, we provided evidence of the effectiveness of distance learning approaches in meeting some of today's challenges. Specifically, we offered evidence of educational effectiveness, business value, cost-effectiveness, and benefits such as linkages to information resources and networks of practicing professionals.

Chapters 2 and 3 were primarily descriptive, providing an overview of the major distance learning technologies in use today. Chapter 2 described some of the older, more traditional—but still effective and widely used—distance learning technologies: audio-conferencing, videoconferencing, and computer-based training. Advanced computer technologies for distance learning were the focus of Chap. 3, which also discussed the impact and implications of this type of distance learning for students as well as instructors.

Chapter 4 was meant to function as an interlude, a time to pause and reflect after the barrage of information about technologies in the first three chapters. That chapter introduced the idea that while technologies are important, they do not in and of themselves constitute distance learning. With all the attention and interest focused on each new technology and technology upgrade as it appears on the scene, it is easy to lose track of the fact that distance learning is more than a collection of hardware: Instead, it is an appropriate combination of people, processes, and technologies. Only by viewing distance learning from this system perspective will you be able to plan, design, and manage distance learning initiatives in ways that maximize their usefulness and effectiveness.

Having established the complex nature of a distance learning system, we moved onto a discussion of the implementation of distance learning programs. Chapters 5, 6, and 7 each provided information and perspectives on different aspects of the process.

Chapter 5 developed the argument that a strong distance learning program must be built on an understanding of the range of organizational and user needs it is expected to meet. For this reason, we recommended that you conduct a thorough analysis of organizational and user needs as well as an assessment of the readiness of individuals and the organization as a whole to adopt this innovation. Also included in Chap. 5 was a discussion of the change process and suggestions for managing it in an organization.

Chapter 6 looked at the equipment, communications services, and facilities that together form the infrastructure of a distance learning project. We described different alternatives and made recommendations about each of those elements as they are applied to audio, video, and Internet-based systems. Chapter 7 examined the heart of the distance learning process: the design, delivery, and evaluation of instruction. We paid particular attention to the modifications that have to be made in moving from traditional instruction to distance instruction: modifications in the development of materials, in instructor skills and techniques, and in assessing the effectiveness of a program.

How to keep things going was the theme of Chap. 8. Once you have a system in place, you need to pay attention to managing day-to-day operations as well as maximizing the use of the system. Scheduling, staffing, promotion, and expansion of the system are aspects of an overall distance learning program that require regular oversight and attention to details. They also require the talents of someone who understands the dynamic nature of both organizational environments and distance learning systems and thus can develop processes in each of those areas that are appropriate for current needs and flexible enough to be adapted for future needs.

Chapter 9 looked at issues in educational institutions. Education and training are often different endeavors, and distance learning programs develop differently in formal educational settings than they do in business and industry. Issues such as scope, focus, and setting influence both the ends a distance learning system is meant to achieve and the ways in which people in the system go about accomplishing those ends. Policy considerations also differ between the two contexts. In higher education, for example, issues of residency, learner support services, and faculty rewards for distance teaching can represent stumbling blocks to the institutional implementation of learning or opportunities to provide evidence of commitment to a distance learning program.

These chapters collectively offered a picture of distance learning as it is today, but what will this process look like tomorrow? For a time it may look much as it does today: Changes will occur, but many will be slow and barely perceptible. Every once in a while, however, there will be a dramatic advancement, a leap forward that clearly highlights the border between the present and the future. The final pages of this book look at the changes we believe will characterize distance learning in the future.

LEARNING IS EVERYWHERE

In tomorrow's communications age learning will no longer be confined within the four walls of a classroom. An instructor armed with a textbook will no longer be the sole source of knowledge and educational experiences. Information resources will be everywhere, often separated from learners by time and space. Distance learning will be the bridge between learners and these distributed learning resources (Fig. 10-1).

Learning is a lifelong pursuit in which training and retraining become strategies for both individual and corporate success. Distance learning will use communications and information technologies to harness the vast array of resources available and stimulate the development of lifelong learning skills. Through distance

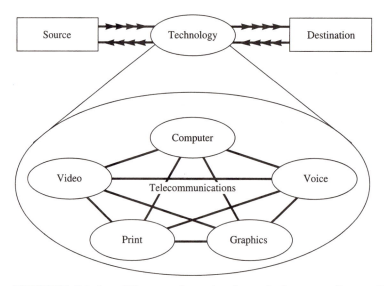

FIGURE 10-1. Distance learning knowledge transfer model.

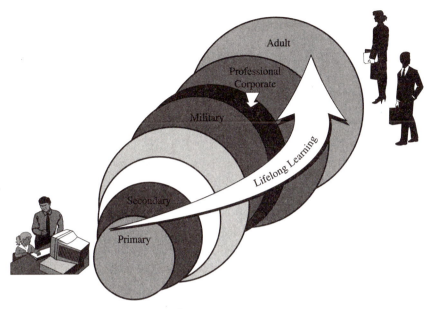

FIGURE 10-2. Distance learning environments.

learning, a variety of audio-, video-, computer-, Internet-, and print-based media will be combined in new and more powerful ways to help learners learn the way they learn best, throughout the life span (Fig. 10-2).

HOW DO PEOPLE LEARN BEST?

Trainers and educators often ask this question. The answer invariably is that it depends on the learning context and the individual's learning style. We as individuals might respond to the question with answers such as "By direct experience," "By experimentation," "By seeing and doing," "By mentoring others," and "By sharing ideas." We might emphasize that we want easy access to relevant information: Getting information when we want it, where we want it, and in a way that is meaningful to us can have significant effects on both our willingness and our ability to learn. Given the changing knowledge needs and the current and projected capabilities of global computer networks, these three requirements should represent the minimum delivery capabilities for a future networked learning environment.

If we reflect for a moment on the traditional twentieth-century educational environment, we shall discover that some of the commonly occurring elements of this context do not match up well with the ways in which most people learn best. In many traditional classrooms students sit and listen to a lecture. The student learns as an individual from an instructor who is viewed as the source of knowledge. The instructor's knowledge and the textbook knowledge are too often viewed as stable content and often are delivered in a homogeneous way for the average student in the audience. The course is considered successful when students demonstrate a mastery of its content by passing an evaluative examination.

While this form is suitable for some types of content and some students, it is often not the most efficient or effective way to learn, especially in workplace environments where there is an expectation that what is learned will be applied immediately to improve performance. Recent work in the cognitive sciences suggests alternative approaches that can enhance learning for many students.

An emerging approach to twenty-first-century learning calls for instruction to become more learner-centered (Fig. 10-3). Networked learning environments will be able to put the learner at the center of the learning experience, that is, connect learners to a rich and varied network of data and human information resources in ways that make them feel they are at the center of that network. Access to both information sources and instructors and others who can provide guidance and support will allow learners to construct knowledge and experiences that are meaningful to them. (What is meaningful, of course, depends on the context and situation. In some instances, learning will be meaningful as it relates to personal growth and

TWENTIETH-CENTURY LEARNING (INSTRUCTOR-CENTERED)	TWENTY-FIRST-CENTURY LEARNING (LEARNER-CENTERED)
Lecture	Facilitation
Individual learning	Team learning
Student as listener	Student as collaborator
Instructor as source	Instructor as guide
Stable content	Dynamic content
Homogeneity	Diversity
Evaluation and testing	Performance

FIGURE 10-3.   A comparison of twentieth-century and twenty-first-century workplace learning environments.

development; in others, as it allows learners to perform their job responsibilities more effectively.)

Increasingly, learning activities can be customized and individually paced to serve a variety of learner needs. In this environment the learner can be less of a listener and more of a collaborator in the learning experience. Technologies that support collaborative work by geographically separated participants will allow team learning, with the learners and instructors sharing responsibility for structuring and maintaining the learning process. As learners gain more experience and confidence in this type of learning environment, the instructor can increasingly fill the role of "guide on the side" rather than "sage on the stage."

In this new learning environment most content is acknowledged to be dynamic rather than static. For this reason, a multiplicity of resources—not just textbooks—are made available to the student to ensure that the content is both up to date and relevant to the learner's situation. The tremendous diversity in the learning resources and activities offered by this learner-centered approach will allow the accommodation of a wide variety of learner needs. A focus on the specific needs of individual learners also will mean that learning outcomes will be more relevant and immediately applicable to improved job performance.

A VISION OF A NETWORKED LEARNING ENVIRONMENT

Our vision of the future of distance learning calls for the creation of networked learning environments that seamlessly integrate voice, video, and data connections between and among learners, instructors, subject matter experts, virtual libraries, Internet resources, and support service organizations. The distance learner is at the center of this network, connected with both real-time and non-real-time links to a wide variety of learning resources. The learning resources are themselves interconnected to form a mosaic of mutually enriching elements (Fig. 10-4).

Networked learning environments have the potential to make education and training more accessible, convenient, focused, effective, and cost-efficient for the learners and the education and training providers. However, to make networked distance learning work well, instructors and providers will need to harness and combine the potential of both synchronous and asynchronous communication technologies.

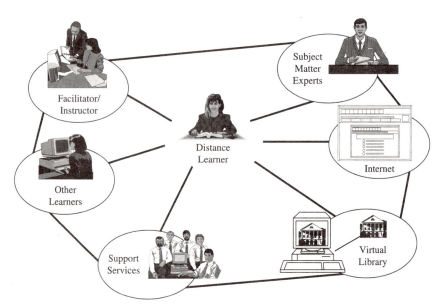

FIGURE 10-4.   Collaborative networked learning environments.

Synchronous video communication technologies such as desktop videoconferencing and interactive group videoconferencing make possible live, real-time interaction between instructors and learners. Instructors, subject matter experts, and learners see and hear each other at all the locations and can engage in interaction similar to that in face-to-face classes. With audioconferencing, the participants engage in real-time dialogue but cannot see those at other sites.

Asynchronous communication technologies support non-real-time interactions and allow access to vast information resources. For example, E-mail communication, chat groups, and on-line forums among instructor, learners, and support services can add opportunities for interaction that extend beyond the actual period during which learners are connected in real time. Multimedia data-bases, virtual libraries, and the Internet make it possible for instruc-tors to store, or "host," large quantities of data, voice, and video resource materials that can be accessed at a time and place conve-nient for the learners.

The challenge will be to implement systems based on the right combination of synchronous and asynchronous technologies to cre-ate networked learning environments that are congruent with the mission of the organization, learner expectations, and the delivery style of the instructor. No single distance learning technology will be able to meet all learning needs; instead, a multiple-media solution will work best for most distance learning implementations.

For example, a desktop video teleconferencing network can link instructor and learners for the presentation and discussion of key course concepts. The data collaboration capabilities of desktop video teleconferencing enable the instructor and the learners to engage in software sharing for the simultaneous editing of documents, completion of budget spreadsheets, or creation of a graphic presentation. Later, learners can continue to discuss ideas with other learners and subject matter experts through an E-mail or chat network. Additional multimedia resources, such as reference articles, journals, magazines, and video news clips, can be accessed from a virtual library or the Internet to supplement and enrich the course content.

Distance learning networks will be used for training, formal education, continuing education, advanced professional education, and management development programs. These networks will improve the reach of programs, stretch education and training dollars, and deliver just-in-time knowledge to learners anywhere and at any time.

In earlier chapters we discussed the effects that distance learning systems are having on instructors, students, learner support personnel, stakeholders, and the organization as a whole. This chapter offers our perspective on the impact of future networked distance learning environments on skills requirements for instructors and the levels of learner support that organizations will have to provide.

NEW SKILLS FOR INSTRUCTORS

The instructor in a networked learning environment will have to become an "orchestrator" of multimedia technologies. Much like the conductor of a symphony orchestra, an instructor calls on media "instruments" such as transparencies, a document camera, videotapes, and computer databases to enhance the presentation. Distance learning delivery is as much an art as a science. To be effective, the instructor needs to think of multiple ways to engage and interact with the learners throughout the synchronous and asynchronous distance learning experience.

As technologies migrate to a higher bandwidth capacity, instructors will be able to deliver the higher audio and video quality that is desirable for many distance learning applications. Fiber-optic technologies often are designed in private networks for increased throughput, reliability, and overall quality. With the deployment of more public Asynchronous Transfer Mode (ATM) technology, many of today's distance learning systems will migrate to broadband ATM networks. Also, broadband multimedia multipoint conferencing units (MCUs) will allow the interoperation of both narrowband and broadband technologies, thus facilitating the growth of higher-bandwidth networks. These developments will expand the options available to instructors and make the distance learning experiences of the future even more engaging and robust than are those available today.

EXPANDED PROVISION OF LEARNER SUPPORT

New instructor skills will have to be complemented by expanded learner support capabilities to maximize the success of the networked learning environment. The student support services organization, that is, the human infrastructure that provides support to distance learners, plays a role similar to that of the customer services operation or call center in a business enterprise. Call centers have sophisticated call management systems that continually monitor the flow of calls into the center, track customer service activities, and provide reports on customer satisfaction. Networked learning environments will need similar management systems that can provide technical troubleshooting, track student progress, and monitor student satisfaction.

For example, in the future there will be learners who are initially uncomfortable with computer technology and may require some type of coaching to help them build their confidence. Learners will expect the network to be easily accessible, running properly, and not distracting in regard to the smooth completion of their course of study. If they have trouble, they will expect someone in a support services role to be available to talk them through the process of registering, logging on, and maintaining access to the network. Even now learners are beginning to expect access to real-time help desk "hot lines" available seven days a week, 16 to 24 hours a day.

This level of customer support is already common in the airline, financial services, and Internet Service Provider industries. The day is fast approaching when education and training providers will be differentiated not only by the quality of their learning materials but also by the level of service they provide to distance learners. By providing comprehensive support services to learners, education and training providers will increase the learners' personal comfort zone with the distance learning environment and allow them to concentrate more on the content and less on the technology.

Training or educational organizations also will need to ensure that their distance learning programs are well designed, clearly describe expected learner outcomes, and are supported by an instructional and student services staff that is available to address program-related comments and concerns. Learners will quickly become frustrated if the information contained in the course material is not accurate and relevant to their needs or if they are unable to progress in accordance with their expectations.

Providers will have to establish a system for gathering student feedback and reporting it to the instructor or course designer to ensure continuous program improvement. They also will need to make provisions for gathering data at the program's end to monitor, evaluate, and improve overall program effectiveness.

ENHANCED LEARNING EXPERIENCES VIA THE INTERNET

More and more, the Internet will become the vehicle on which training and educational organizations rely to support enhanced learning experiences for their distant students. Its expanded communications capabilities and breadth of resources have the potential to enrich all facets of the teaching and learning process.

Internet Communications. The Internet is now the preferred method for communication between distance learners and their instructors. Learners like the ability to ask questions at a time and place convenient to their needs. Some learners have even reported that Internet-based courses offer them more access to their instructors and other learners than do face-to-face courses. Internet communications also have the potential to connect learners to support services, librarians, and subject matter experts other than the instructor. As distance learning programs become more firmly integrated into the mainstream of the organizations they serve, such linkages will both expand and become accepted as part of an organization's responsibility to provide equitable services and resources to all learners.

Course Content Hosting. Incorporating multimedia information and presentations hosted on the Internet into learning experiences provides students with a variety of channels through which to receive and process information. The audio, video, and data interactions that result offer simulating learning experiences that complement more traditional forms of content presentation, such as textbooks. Currently, access to some of the newer Web-hosted presentational materials, such as streaming audio and video, is difficult or impossible for some students, particularly those with older or less powerful computers. However, technological advances and falling prices are combining to bring such resources within the reach of increasing numbers of distant learners. Again, we see today's cutting edge becoming tomorrow's mainstream.

Student Testing.   Educational and training organizations often need to make sure that learning has occurred. Currently, testing on the Internet can be accomplished by using familiar evaluation instruments such as true-false, multiple-choice, and/or matching tests. Instructors using an Internet-based testing system can quickly create evaluation exercises or instruments that learners can access and complete when and where it is convenient. Test results and evaluative comments can be posted for easy and private access by learners.

Some instructors worry that students may collaborate on Internet-based tests when they are not physically in the presence of the instructor. Actually, such collaboration can be a very positive learning activity as students share knowledge and different viewpoints on a subject, thus enhancing their individual learning.

However, there are situations in which examination security is necessary. Today the most common approach is for the instructor to require students to take examinations in a proctored testing setting, using the Internet only for practice quizzes or self-assessments. Innovative course management tools for the Internet are offering instructors new alternatives, however. Some applications allow instructors to generate quizzes and examinations made up of questions randomly selected from a master list and different for each student. In this way, each member of a class of 20 students at a distant site can have completely different but related questions to answer. These Internet-based student evaluation systems can be designed to provide learners with immediate test results and recommended links to remedial activities. New advances in technology, particularly applications related to those which allow secure financial transactions, may soon offer instructors other options for ensuring testing and evaluation security.

Virtual Libraries.   Just as the campus library today provides on-campus students with an extensive repository of indexed information, the virtual library of the future will provide seamlessly integrated voice, video, and data resources for distant learners. As more powerful electronic technologies are used to support various forms of distance learning, virtual libraries will grow and become more multifaceted. These libraries will allow organizations to incorporate multimedia "artifacts" from sources worldwide into networked teaching and learning exercises.

As enhanced media archiving technologies become available, instructors will have to learn the most effective ways to incorporate these knowledge resources into their multimedia virtual libraries. They also will have to be able to show learners how to create their own personalized virtual libraries by "bookmarking" Web site resources. With appropriate guidance, the students will become active researchers, first searching for and then sharing with other learners dynamic Web-based content that will enrich the learning experience. The Web resources that students bookmark will remain available and useful to them long after they complete the formal training program. Instructors and training organizations alike need to begin thinking about and planning for ways to capitalize on the current and emerging capabilities of Internet-based virtual learning for their students.

NETWORKED LEARNING ENVIRONMENT SCENARIOS

In this section we have created sample scenarios for future networked learning environments defined by the dimensions of time and space (*Table 10-1*). Each of these environments presents issues of delivery as well as session preservation or archiving, which allows it to be delivered later to others or stored for use as reference material. Recording, storing, and indexing sessions or portions of sessions for later retrieval are all aspects of creating and maintaining networked learning environments.

TABLE 10-1. Networked Learning Scenarios

Scenario	Time of Event for All Learners	Location of Event for All Learners
1	Same time	Same place
2	Same time	Different place
3	Different time	Same place
4	Different time	Different place

Scenario 1.   Scenario 1 (same time, same place) depicts a "typical" face-to-face learning environment, which will continue to be appropriate or even necessary for some content and some learner populations. In this scenario, the learners and the instructor are all located in the same place and the training session occurs within the same time frame for all the participants. In other ways, this face-to-face learning environment will be less typical. It may be complemented by presession assignments or readings distributed by E-mail or hosted in a multimedia database, or students may give presentations to peers during a face-to-face session into which they incorporate prerecorded sources or choose to go "live" on the Internet to access and share Web-based resources.

Scenario 2.   Scenario 2 (same time, different place) describes a synchronous distance learning environment. Learners and instructor are not all at the same location but gather at the same time for learning activities and interaction. Audioconferencing and videoconferencing remain common technologies for bridging the gap between instructors and learners, but this purpose also may be accomplished by collaborative data—computer—conferencing. Students participate in multimedia learning experiences and active collaboration in which they share common software applications with instructors and fellow students. Instructors can conduct the multipoint, multimedia teleconferences by using Integrated Services Digital Network (ISDN) lines or connections via local area network/wide area network (LAN/WAN) or Internet/intranet.

Scenario 3.   Scenario 3 (different time, same place) describes a "learning lab" type of environment. Learners who were not present during the "live" session in the laboratory, museum, or classroom come at a later time to the place where the program was conducted to "experience" it. Various recording technologies, including Web-based multimedia content hosting, enable students to participate in a virtual classroom experience hours or days after it originally occurred. The students experience a recorded session but still can actively interact with the content and with other learners through asynchronous E-mail communications and simulations. For example, a learner may send his or her session notes to the other learners on the network for review and comment or may arrange to collaborate with other learners in completing a simulation activity on equipment in the learning lab.

Scenario 4. In Scenario 4 (different time, different place) the learner accesses the information or learning activity not only at a later time but also from a different location. The instructor and the students may never actually meet in real time or space, yet they share ideas and learning occurs in their virtually shared space. Communications with others in the learning group may be accomplished with asynchronous technologies, including E-mail and bulletin boards, allowing threaded discussions.

Scenario 4 may include other forms of education and training, such as computer-based training (CBT) and electronic performance support systems (EPSSs), which were discussed in Chaps. 2 and 3, respectively. When bandwidths are limited, the Internet/intranet can be used as a distribution medium for CBT, with courses being downloaded for storage and execution on the learner's personal computer (PC). With increases in bandwidth, networks will be able to run multimedia state-of-the-art CBT programs. Examinations and interaction with the instructor and other students will be conducted via asynchronous communications.

In an EPSS the learner interacts with an electronic "mentor" to obtain advice and guidance on the performance of a task. When confronted with difficulties in completing a task, the learner enters data into his or her computer, asking the EPSS for assistance. The system interprets questions, generates responses, and prescribes training modules that will be useful to the learner. A sophisticated EPSS is adaptive; that is, it prescribes the modules that best match the learning style and preferences of the individual learner. It keeps track of what the learner already knows, and a "wizard" suggests help when it detects that the learner is having difficulty. For example, the learner may be an investment adviser trying to determine what long-term savings option makes the most sense for a client on the basis of just-implemented tax law changes. The learner can complete a training module, put information into an expert system, get advice, see examples, and create a proposal to present to the client. The EPSS "mentors" the learner and streamlines the process the learner follows to perform the job task.

The Future of Networked Learning Environments

The challenge of creating networked learning environments is to determine what learners truly need and how to accommodate their needs. The future will include all the technological capabilities described in this book and more: three-dimensional presentations, artificial intelligence, and virtual reality, for example. Learners, instructors, and educational and training organizations will have incredibly rich options for determining how to create, manage, and experience learning.

Our fledgling distance learning networks, Internet experiences, and virtual library initiatives foreshadow future networked learning environments. Simple functions such as the bookmark feature of Internet browsers will be dramatically extended to allow bookmarking of virtual journeys in an electronic world. Intelligent "agents" that "remember" learners' interests and requirements will assist in locating and navigating through the most relevant virtual libraries. These intelligent agents will sustain learning experiences in a virtual learning space, allowing learners to re-create and reexperience learning events, activities, and simulations.

Future networked learning environments will run the gamut from a single training department solution, to an enterprisewide solution, to massive educational utilities with knowledge resources built on years of collaboration and partnering among many training and education providers. Many technological and pedagogical challenges will have to be addressed along the way. We will need new and more powerful tools to store voice, video, and data; facilitate the identification of appropriate resources; and present resources in forms characterized by seamless interoperability among multiple systems. Other needed tools will include information-indexing agents, search engines, expert systems, scenario builders, massive multimedia storage systems, and broadband multimedia networks. These tools will allow the development of successful learning environments that are easy to use, effective, appealing to the learner, affordable, and flexible enough to accommodate rapid change.

Technology has had a dramatic impact on how we work, entertain ourselves, live our lives, and learn; it can be expected to continue to do so in the future. We know that technology-based distance learning is not the solution to every educational and training challenge, but the search for solutions must incorporate a consideration of the technologies that not only are offering new and more powerful ways to communicate but are completely reshaping modern life. We need to start now—with intention and vision—on our journey along the evolutionary and revolutionary path to creating future networked learning environments. Learning is everything—make it happen!

FOR FURTHER REFERENCE

Chute, A. G., B. W. Hancock, and L. B. Balthazar. 1991. Distance education futures: Information needs and technology options. *Performance and Instruction* (November–December).

Chute, A. G., P. K. Sayers, and R. P. Gardner. 1997. Teaching and learning at a distance: What it takes to effectively design, deliver and evaluate programs. In T. E. Cyrs (ed.). *New directions for teaching and learning*, Number 71, pp. 75–83, San Francisco: Jossey-Bass.

Davis, S., and J. Botkin. 1994. *The monster under the bed: How business is mastering the opportunity*, New York: Simon & Schuster.

Gates, B. 1995. *The road ahead*, New York: Viking.

Grove, A. S. 1996. *Only the paranoid survive: How to exploit the crisis points that challenge every company and leader*, New York: Doubleday.

Johansen, R., et. al. 1988. *Groupware: Computer support for business teams*, New York: Free Press–Macmillan.

Mehlinger, H. D. 1995. *School reform in the information age*, Newtown, Penn.: Media Management.

Moore, M. G. (ed.). 1990. *Contemporary issues in American distance education*, New York: Pergamon Press.

Negroponte, N. 1995. *Being digital*, New York: Knopf.

Stolovitch, H. D., and E. J. Keeps (eds.). 1992. *Handbook of human performance technology*, San Francisco: Jossey-Bass.

Sullivan, G., and T. Rocco. 1996. *Guiding principles for distance learning in a learning society*, Washington, D.C.: American Council on Education.

Thompson, M. M., and A. C. Chute. 1996. A vision for distance education: Networked learning environments. *Open Learning* 13(2).

GLOSSARY

Analog: Continuously varying in frequency and amplitude. Televisions and telephones have traditionally used analog technology to re-create voices and pictures. Analog technology is much slower and has poorer quality than does the digital technology that is rapidly replacing it.

Application sharing: A feature supported by many desktop videoconferencing systems that allows the participants at both ends of a videoconference to view and edit the same computer application or document.

Asynchronous communication: Interaction between two or more people that is time-delayed, that is, separated by minutes, hours, or even days. Correspondence courses and E-mail are asynchronous forms of distance learning. The opposite is *synchronous communication,* such as talking on the phone or videoconferencing. Good distance learning programs typically use both synchronous and asynchronous communication.

Audioconferencing: Voice communications, traditionally accomplished by using standard telephone lines, although new technologies, such as Internet telephony are gaining a portion of the market. When more than one person is in a single location, speakerphones or special audioconference terminal equipment is employed. When more than two locations are involved, multipoint bridging equipment or Internet-based software is used.

Audiographics: Teleconferencing that interconnects graphic display devices, such as computer monitors, located at sites separated by a distance. The technology generally allows the participants to view the same high-resolution [Video Graphic Array (VGA) or better] still-frame visual at each site. Some systems allow annotation, writing, or drawing on the screen.

Basic rate interface (BRI): A digital communications circuit with 128 Kbit/s of bandwidth. Integrated Services Digital Network (ISDN) BRI circuits can send three digital signals over a single pair of copper wires: two voice (B) channels and one signal (D) channel.

Broadband: Refers to high-capacity communications circuit, usually with a speed greater than 1.544 Mbit/s.

Business television (BTV): A technology that employs one-way motion-video from an origination site to multiple receiving sites. Used when it is not important to the content or message to see participants at the receiving sites. Receiving sites generally are provided with a way to respond to the origination site, usually by audioconference (voice), a response system or facsimile. Common transmission systems include satellites and Instructional Television Fixed Service (ITFS).

Coder-decoder (CODEC): Videoconferencing hardware that codes the outgoing video and audio signals and decodes the incoming signals. Before transmission, a CODEC converts analog signals to digital signals and compresses the digital signals. Incoming audio and video signals must be decompressed and converted from digital back to analog.

Compressed video: When the vast amount of information in a normal television transmission is squeezed into a fraction of its former bandwidth by a CODEC, the resulting compressed video can be transmitted more economically over a smaller carrier. Some information is sacrificed in the process, and this may result in diminished picture and sound quality.

Desktop videoconferencing: Videoconferencing on a personal computer; most appropriate for small groups or individuals. Many desktop videoconferencing systems support document sharing.

Digital: Refers to information stored in a binary language of ones and zeros. Computer technology is digital. Audio/video signals are represented by discrete variations (in voltage, frequency, amplitude, location, etc.). In general, digital signals can be transmitted faster and more accurately than can analog signals. For example, music from digital CDs is usually more clear than music from analog records.

Distance learning: A system and a process of connecting learners with distributed learning resources. This definition is from the American Council on Education (ACE).

Distance learning system: An integrated combination of technologies designed to support interactive teaching and learning among persons not physically present in the same location. Such systems often emphasize one technology but draw on others for increased flexibility. For example, a system built on video as the primary method of delivery may use voice mail, E-mail, Internet multimedia databases, and fax technologies to provide additional interaction between and support for the participants.

Full-motion video: Equivalent to broadcast television video with a frame rate of 30 frames per second. Images are sent in real time, and motion is continuous.

H.320 standard: A widely used video compression standard that allows a variety of videoconferencing systems to communicate. This standard was approved by the International Telecommunications Union (ITU).

Interaction: The communication or dialogue that occurs between instructors and learners or among learners. May be time-delayed (asynchronous) or real-time (synchronous). Examples of asynchronous interaction include correspondence, voice mail, and computer E-mail. Synchronous interaction can occur by telephone, audioconferencing, videoconferencing, and Internet telephony.

Integrated Services Digital Network (ISDN): A digital network that provides communications of voice, video, and data between desktop videoconferencing systems, group videoconferencing systems, and computers.

Multimedia: Refers to a combination of audio, video, and/or computer technologies that provide a range of expression and experience.

Multipoint conferencing unit (MCU): A device that allows three or more sites to interact actively during a video teleconference. Each site must connect via an MCU, similar to the way sites on an audio teleconference connect to an audio bridge.

Narrowband: Refers to a low-capacity communications circuit that usually has a speed of 56 Kbit/s or less.

Networking: The connecting of multiple sites for the transfer and/or exchange of information via computers.

Networked virtual learning environment: Simulated educational activities and structures that so closely match the real event that they seem almost real or give students the feeling of actually "being there." For example, instructors and students who meet and collaborate only electronically are not really in a classroom together. However, a well-designed virtual learning environment can use the power and flexibility of communications technologies to simulate or substitute for many of the aspects of classroom instruction.

On line: Being in direct communication with a remote computer or computer system, thus enabling communication and/or transfer or exchange of information.

Synchronous communication: An interaction between individuals or groups that occurs at the same time, that is, with no appreciable delay between the end of one message and the beginning of another. Face-to-face, telephone, and video teleconference conversations are synchronous.

T.120 standard: A standard that supports audiographics and desktop conferencing between platforms. Standards-based systems support desktop conferencing, application and document sharing, and collaboration.

Teleconferencing: The use of electronic channels to facilitate communication among groups of people at two or more locations. *Teleconferencing* is a generic term that refers to a variety of technologies and applications. Technologies include but are not limited to POTS (plain old telephone service), ISDN, satellite, Internet local area network/wide area network (LAN/WAN), T1, and DS-3. Applications include but are not limited to telemeetings, telecollaboration, telecommuting, distance education, and teletraining. This definition is from the International Teleconferencing Association (ITCA).

Videoconferencing: Similar in concept to audioconferencing but employs both voice and motion-video communications. Participants are able to see participants at other locations if allowed by the chairperson or instructor. Uses digital transmission systems such as ISDN, switched 56 services, or dedicated channels such as DS-3 and fiber optics.

Web site: A location on the World Wide Web that is accessed by instructing the computer to find and connect to the site's specific Internet address, known as its uniform resource locator (URL). Web sites are repositories of information about a specific topic, institution, organization, person, place, or thing.

World Wide Web (WWW): Also known as the Web. A virtual library of video, audio, and textual data and information stored on the computers of the Internet. These data are accessible to anyone with a modem, a personal computer, a way of connecting to the Internet (through a private or public Internet Service Provider), and a computer application program or "software" called a browser designed to allow a person to explore Web resources.

VENDORS

Throughout this book we have described technologies that support the implementation of audio, audiographic, video, and Internet distance learning systems. The existing technologies are continually changing, and new technologies are introduced annually. We felt that the most appropriate way to provide up-to-date information was to direct you to current listings of vendors in the distance learning field.

We have secured permission from the International Teleconferencing Association (ITCA) and the University of Wisconsin–Extension Distance Education Clearinghouse to direct you to their listings of technology vendors. The ITCA maintains a listing of teleconferencing vendors that are sustaining members of the ITCA. That site can be accessed at http://www.itca.org/, and the vendor list can be accessed directly at http://www.itca.org/expo.

The University of Wisconsin–Extension Distance Education Clearinghouse provides a comprehensive listing of vendors that provide a wide variety of distance learning products and services. The Distance Education Clearinghouse gave us permission to provide excerpts from its listing of technology vendors, which was current at the time this book was published.

DISTANCE LEARNING TECHNOLOGY PRODUCT AND SERVICE VENDORS

The following list was developed by the Distance Education Clearinghouse World Wide Web site (http://www.uwex.edu/disted/vendor.htm), University of Wisconsin–Extension, copyright 1998.

- *ACT Teleconferencing* (http://www.acttel.com)

223

ACT Teleconferencing provides audio, video, and data conferencing products and services.

- *ADC Telecommunications* (http://www.adc.com)
  ADC is a supplier of transmission and networking systems for telecommunications, cable television, broadcast, wireless, and enterprise networks.

- *Ameritech* (http://www.ameritech.com)
  In addition to providing Illinois, Indiana, Michigan, Ohio, and Wisconsin with local telephone service, Ameritech offers cellular, long-distance, paging, cable television, security monitoring, electronic commerce, managed services, and wireless data communications for much of the United States and many parts of Europe.

- *Apple Computer, Inc.* (http://www.apple.com)
  Apple develops, manufactures, licenses, and markets solutions, products, technologies, and services for business, education, consumer, entertainment, scientific and engineering, and government customers.

- *AT&T* (http://www.att.com)
  The AT&T Learning Network provides the latest technology to schools and communities as well as support and information on how to plan for and use technology effectively.

- *British Telecommunications* (BT) (http://www.bt.com)
  Includes information about BT, and its Internet access program, information about BT products, and details of the research being conducted at the BT Laboratories.

- *Chaparral Communications, Inc.* (http://www.chaparral.net)
  Chaparral provides products used in commercial and residential satellite reception systems worldwide.

- *Cisco Systems, Inc.* (http://www.cisco.com)
  The Cisco Education Network describes Cisco's education programs and upcoming events and the use of the Internet in schools.

- *Compunetix* (http://www.compunetix.com)
  Compunetix designs, manufactures, markets, installs, operates, and supports a new generation of high-performance digital teleconferencing systems.

- *ConferTech International, Inc.* (http://www.confertech.com)
  ConferTech International, Inc., is a dedicated multimedia teleconferencing company that markets equipment and services worldwide.

- *Convergent Media Systems* (http://www.convergent.com)
  Convergent's interactive distance learning package includes real-time remote interactivity, multimedia support materials available on demand to the presenter, viewer interactive keypads with a built-in microphone, and training and development program content.

- *DataBeam* (http://www.databeam.com)
  DataBeam develops and markets multimedia communications technology. Its products range from application software, to servers, to developers' tool kits for the Internet and dial-up networks, including products such as FarSite and the new T.120 Conference Server.

- *Executone Information Systems, Inc.* (http://www.executone.com)
  Executone designs, markets, and supports a comprehensive line of communications products and services for computer telephony, call center management, and health care communications.

- *Force, Incorporated* (http://www.forceinc.com)
  Force, Incorporated, manufactures fiber-optic video, audio, and data links as well as fiber-optic test equipment for the data communication and telecommunication industries and the military.

- *FTP Software, Inc.* (http://www.ftp.com)
  FTP Software, Inc., provides open, secure, managed IP client and server network applications, along with services that allow customers to access host and server-based information regardless of computer hardware, operating system, or physical location.

- *Gentner Communications Corporation* (http://www.gentner.com)
  Gentner develops and manufactures audio solutions for the broadcast, teleconferencing, and assistive listening markets. Its mission is to help build synergistic relationships between people who are geographically separated by providing customers with total audio solutions.

- *GlobeCast* (http://www.keystonecom.com)
  GlobeCast is a U.S.-based value-added provider of transmission services for video, audio, and broadcast data applications.

- *GTE* (http://www.gte.com)
  GTE is made up of many business units throughout the United States, with operations that extend throughout the world. GTE's distance learning solutions include implementing the appropriate technology and the latest distance learning conventions.

- *Hitachi (HSC) Canada Inc., Multimedia Division*

(http://www.hitachi.com)
Products include computer monitors, personal computers (PCs), televisions, digital boards, hand-held PCs, liquid crystal display projectors, video printers, and cameras.

- *IBM* (http://www.ibm.com)
Higher Education—IBM Global Campus combines advanced technologies, network computing solutions, applications, consulting, and services tailored to enable colleges and universities to expand their offerings to new groups of students. The K-12 Solutions—IBM K-12 Education site offers news, solutions, technical information, and a teachers corner.

- *LearningSpace* (http://www.lotus.com/learningspace)
LearningSpace is Lotus's technology for creating and delivering education and training. It combines any time, anywhere distance learning with the face-to-face classroom benefits of a rich, collaborative, instructor-facilitated environment.

- *Lucent Technologies* (http://www.lucent.com/cedl)
Lucent Technologies designs, builds and delivers a wide range of public and private networks, communications systems and software, consumer and business telephone systems, and microelectronics components. Bell Laboratories is the research and development arm of the company. The Center for Excellence in Distance Learning provides information on state-of-the-art distance learning technologies and applications.

- *MCI* (http://www.mci.com)
MCI provides network conferencing, audioconferencing, videoconferencing, and document conferencing services. The distance learning center can help in designing a specific distance learning program, including course planning and expert consultation, by conducting classes and course evaluations "virtually."

- *Microsoft* (http://www.microsoft.com)
Microsoft offers a wide range of products and services for business and personal use designed to take advantage of the full power of personal computing.

- *MultiLink* (http://www.multilink.com)
MultiLink's audioconferencing products are used by commercial, education, government, and service provider organizations for applications that include business meetings, shareholder services, public relations, project management, focus groups, teletraining, distance learning, and crisis management.

- *NEC America, Inc.* (http://www.nec.com)
  NEC America, Inc., an affiliate of NEC Corporation, develops, manufactures, and markets communications products and software for public and private networks, including digital key telephone and private branch exchange systems, Asynchronous Transfer Mode (ATM) switching systems, PCS equipment, cellular telephones, pagers, facsimile equipment, videoconferencing equipment, fiber-optic transmission systems, data communications products, digital microwave radio, satellite communications, and network management systems.

- *Nortel (Northern Telecom)* (http://www.nortel.com)
  Nortel works with customers in more than 150 countries to design, build, and integrate communications products and advanced digital networks. Nortel's distance learning turnkey solutions include hardware and software such as video coders-decoders (CODECs), ATM access multiplexers, data ports, transmission equipment, control cabinets and racks, power supplies, cables and connectors, room preparation and integration, installation, training, and service.

- *Novell* (http://www.novell.com)
  Novell provides network software. The company offers a wide range of network solutions for distributed network, Internet, intranet, and small-business markets. Novell offers comprehensive education and technical support programs.

- *Pacific Bell Network* (http://www.pacbell.com)
  The Pacific Bell Knowledge Network Explorer offers a wide spectrum of products, services, and programs to educators, including the Pacific Bell Education First initiative that helps schools and libraries connect to the information superhighway.

- *PictureTel* (http://www.picturetel.com)
  PictureTel develops, manufactures, and markets a full range of videoconferencing solutions. It also markets network conferencing servers and a comprehensive portfolio of enterprisewide services, providing videoconferencing solutions to customers in the distance learning, health care, financial services, and manufacturing industries.

- *Polycom, Inc.* (http://www.polycom.com)
  Polycom develops, manufactures, and markets audioconferencing and data conferencing products that facilitate meetings at a distance.

- *Question Mark Testing and Surveying*
  (http://www.questionmark.com)
  Question Mark enables teachers and trainers to write, administer, and mark tests by using computers and the World Wide Web.

- *Shure Brothers Incorporated* (http://www.shure.com)
  Shure is a leader in the microphone business, with consumer and professional products that meet a variety of audio applications from quality phonography cartridges, to world-standard stage performance microphones, to problem-solving mixers, to teleconferencing products.

- *Sprint Communications Company* (http://www.sprint.com)
  Sprint works closely with the industry's most stable and respected suppliers of videoconferencing technology and equipment.

- *Street Technologies, Inc.* (http://www.streetinc.com)
  Street enables users to view synchronized audio, video, graphic animation, and text across intranets, local area networks, and the Internet.

- *Sun Microsystems, Inc.* (http://www.sun.com)
  Sun provides hardware, software, and services for establishing enterprisewide network solutions, offering products from JAVA smart cards to SPARC supercomputers.

- *TeleSpan: A Bulletin on Teleconferencing* (http://www.telespan.com)
  Elliot Gold founded TeleSpan in 1981 as a publishing and consulting company in the area of teleconferencing.

- *Teletraining Institute* (http://www.teletrain.com)
  The Teletraining Institute provides training for distance educators and offers workshops, courses, and academies.

- *UOL, Publishing, Inc.* (http://www.uol.com)
  UOL is a publisher of interactive, Web-based courseware delivered through the Internet or corporate intranets to the education and training market.

- *VSI Enterprises, Inc.* (http://www.vsin.com)
  VSI designs, manufactures, markets, and supports an array of videoconferencing products, along with integrated telecommunications software and services, including product applications designed for use in distance education.

- *VStream* (http://www.vstream.com)
  VStream provides video on demand and audio on demand services to corporations worldwide. VStream collects, digitally

encodes, and stores a company's media content from various sources, such as videotape, audioconferencing or videoconferencing, and satellite reception.

- *VTEL* (http://www.vtel.com)
  VTEL's digital visual communication systems are deployed in corporations, health care facilities, educational institutions, and government operations around the globe. VTEL technology is utilized for distance education.

INDEX

INDEX

ABOUT THE AUTHORS

ALAN CHUTE, PH.D., is the director of the Center for Excellence in Distance Learning at Lucent Technologies: Bell Labs Innovations. Dr. Chute developed the AT&T National Training Center and Teletraining Networks, which won the 10-Year Distinguished Service to the Industry award from the United States Distance Learning Association. With over 25 years of professional experience in distance learning, Dr. Chute has authored over 50 articles on a range of subjects, including advanced learning systems, reengineering the training organization, and the future of distance learning. He has also taught at the university level and was director of a statewide medical distance learning program.

MELODY THOMPSON, ED.D., is a staff writer and editor for the American Journal of Distance Education. She earned her doctorate at Penn State University in adult education, with an emphasis on distance learning.

BURTON HANCOCK, PH.D., is training director at Nationwide Insurance, with training responsibility for more than 20,000 agents. Much of that training is delivered via the Internet. A former senior manager at Ernst & Young, he directed training for their business process reengineering. He also worked for AT&T, where he developed computer-based training, online testing, and performance support tools.